EXACTING CLAM No. 11 — Winter 2023

C000272006

CONTENTS

2	Guillermo Stitch	From the Editor
4	Jake Goldsmith	Distrust and Expertise—A Brief Note
6	Melissa McCarthy	*Hola*, Zinedine
11	Thomas Walton	Unsavory Thoughts
14	Kevin Boniface	Natural History
16	Paolo Pergola	The Comet Star
17	Tomoé Hill	Scents of Grace
19	Kurt Luchs	Ah, Did You Once See Borges Plain?
23	Kurt Luchs	Two After Borges
24	Henrietta Goodman	GG Allin Made Me Write This
34	Megan Catana	Father Dad
39	Alvin Krinst	A Passing Fit
40	Niamh Mac Cabe	The Cailleach's Loch
44	Jack Foley	The McLuriad
50	Jim Meirose	The Ball Is in Your Court Now, Paris!
52	DS Maolalai	Two Poems
53	PJ Blumenthal	Three Poems
56	Dave Drayton	noob boon
57	Akshat Khare	The Taste of Limes
58	Kent Kosack	Formula for Elephants
65	Ben Libman	Will the Circle Be Unbroken
69	Glenn Ingersoll	A Window
70	Daniel Felsenthal	Six Poems
79	Nick Holdstock	Adults
83	REYoung	Beauty
85	Hélène Sanguinetti	"I took 3 cows to the countryside" (tr. Ann Cefola)
87	Oisín Breen	Five Poems
90	David Ricchiute	Standing Perfectly Still on the Table
92	Marvin Cohen	Loving Candace
94	Vincent Czyz	Contrary Star
100	Mike Silverton	Ten Acuities
103	Jesi Bender	Reviews: Oisín Breen's *Lilies on the Deathbed of Étaín and Other Poems*, Dan O'Brien's *Survivor's Notebook*, Sophie Klahr & Corey Zeller's *There is Only One Ghost in the World*
106	M.J. Nicholls	Alexander Theroux's *Later Stories*
108	David Kuhnlein	CJ Christine's *F20 Grail 12*
109	Charles Holdefer	Curtis Smith's *The Lost and the Blind*
111	Debra Di Blasi	Epistles of the Unsaintly
112	Christopher Boucher	Joyreaders

Front cover: "Have a Very Clammy Christmas" by Tyler C. Gore

Quintagrams in black boxes by **Richard Kostelanetz**. Interior art by **Roísin Ní Neachtain** (page 2) and **Jesse Hilson** (page 49).

© 2023 Sagging Meniscus Press
All Rights Reserved

ISBN: 978-1-952386-86-2

exactingclam.com

Exacting Clam is a quarterly publication from Sagging Meniscus.

Contributing Editors: Jake Goldsmith, Tomoé Hill, Kurt Luchs, Melissa McCarthy, M.J. Nicholls, Thomas Walton

Contributing Metaclamician: Christopher Boucher

Senior Editors: Jeff Chon, Elizabeth Cooperman, Tyler C. Gore, Doug Nufer

Fiction Editor: Charles Holdefer • *Poetry Editor:* Aaron Anstett • *Reviews Editor:* Jesi Bender

Executive Editor: Guillermo Stitch

Publisher: Jacob Smullyan

Guillermo Stitch

From the Editor

What follows consists, I'm delighted to claim, of a thousand and one:

The last gristly bear of the norn iron prolapse, fellas. That's what's in steak. Peas processed, pureé on tedium high. A cure for begrudgery, porridge etc. Hardly roquette science. This is all best done when the head is loose and lively lazy. Swing low sweet escariot. Come in for the dooby. The do do. A day without danger. A fib in the head. Charles Holdefer has been in touch: while it is true that I am the harbinger of perhaps the largest stash of plastic tarp in the country (Belgium) this does not make me a concealer of dogs. I celebrate the canine. You are wel-come to check the pit. Many thanks, Charles. Keep us posted. Apples are nice, aren't they? *Aren't they?* Boiled sweets' best flavour. Just an opinion. A snail on ˙the loathsome spine. A suite of virgins huddle disgustingly around the urinal. Nuts. Duchamp apoplectic. Checkmate in poo. Mushroom media. Medial crania. Beetle mania. Judy? Judy? Judy? Judy! La la la la la la la l'aglio. Stanlio e Ollio is a household favourite but it's tricky—if you don't grate the cheese finely enough and stir it in at exactingly the right moment the sauce will split. El gordo y el flaco. Harrowing memories of Korea. Oh, unhappy helicopter! I am woke at night. It isn't easy. Navigate the limelight. Rouse the chancery. In the day I rail against progress, empaths and sensible attitudes to wealth distribution. Peace cake. Don't mind if I do do. Oriental choo choo—enough of Stan and his bull, the chaplain is here. Be slowly, stupid. Medium session ale. Not the same. Never the same

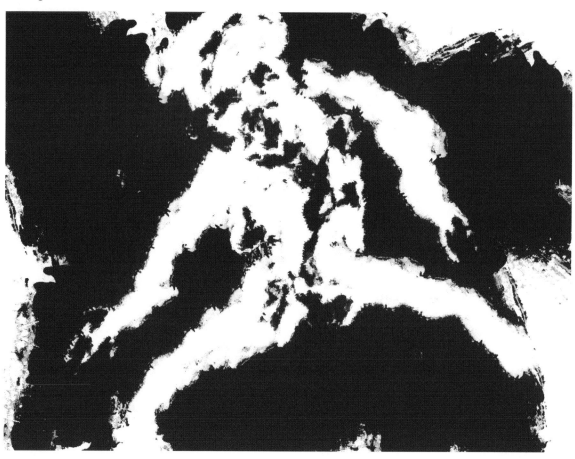

same, always the twain. Or mostly. Ding dong. Young Arenaceous Nell had never once in his life seen the sea, never mind have it fill his nostrils with its salty perfume or his head with the bellow of its heaving waters. Not once had he heard the slap of waves against a quay till that morning, long ago, when he'd watched them send a spray in high spumes over the top; still less have it toss him bodily about as he clutched the gunwale with one hand and his hat, in great peril of getting blown away by a high wind, in the other. There was the distinct possibility, at any moment, of his losing his balance entirely and of tumbling directly into the lap of one of his companions. The two adjacent, both of them ladies, had their hands to the their mouths, so aghast were they at the prospect. A hokusai mount, a red raw nipple, a raving whorl. Babylon fortress. The Qasr al-Sham. The city has grown in the days since, sprawling the Muqattam. Spillage and spoil in pieces of time. A large canton in the skeptical aisle, all over the war. The costumers are slipping. Complaint forms are always available for those who might request. Almost always. The glance of her jet black eyes was that of a gazelle, quarry of noblemen. He had seen the graceful movement of her limbs which were like flowering branches. The words that fell from her lips were the headiest musk, the coolest water and the finest wine, causing him to recite the following lines. There seems to have been some kind of misunderstanding. Write an editorial they said. It'll be fine they said. I conceived in the last days of summer, the lazy, listless days of high heat, bare feet held over the edge of a hammock to catch the breeze, nobody thinking straight, any notion of the long view lost in the shimmer of empty, endless afternoons. Perhaps the brutalities of her own people's past were too recent. In my defence, she had been passed through every psychfilter required of Brigade householders and no concerns had arisen. Her sense of humour had raised an eyebrow here and

there but was not without precedent and appeared firmly rooted in experiential observation (for the purposes of irony), self-deprecation in the face of inadequate daily task performance and so on. We would ride out the pony hers the trap mine arenaceous at the reins sometimes her never me never mind would take the middle seat I would my excuse the hamper best place to have it on the lap cheese sandwiches and pilfered wine and she to my left or my right and he to my right or my left the silken arcs of their cooing and courting would cocoon me didn't mind that wasn't left out not entirely for he wasn't always as charming as he himself believed or as clever not quite the dashing scapegrace he thought himself and when she thought him stupid when one of his little cupids missed its mark her lips would tighten to suppress the smile that would shine instead from her eye when she winked at me. Herr Benjamin Bourbaki begs of the Noble Burgers of Einpferd that they ready themselves for a Magnificent Revelation on The Wahrberg. Time & date to be announced with perhaps as little as some hours notice but almost certainly in June. And now she was the storm. And now, for just a moment, Clara again. And now a bird over the pear tree. Her eye closed and she was Clara, opened and she was the bird. Closed, Clara. Open, the storm. Closed—now she was someone called Lita. Open—she was Dembe. And now she was Sharazad. And now, the bird again. Now Clara, now not. Sharazad. Lita. Clara. And Rolf's arm was tight, and began to lift her and there was still the smell of burning, despite the wet and the wind. Someone screamed. And someone else. And no, she wouldn't die. She would live. Because they needed her. The boys for the stories. Lia. Because Mila was so utterly dependent on her, and was waiting for her. Holdefer's been leaving notes: da do do do da da da da. You're not helping, Charles. There appears to have been some kind of mistake.

Jake Goldsmith

Distrust and Expertise—A Brief Note

First, I have to give some credit to the philosopher Vlad Vexler, who I recommend as a sound analyst of political philosophy, as well as the late Bernard Williams—of whom Vexler is also an admirer. I can't claim to have much in the way of original thought and I repeat from memory some of what they might also say, or would hopefully agree with. So I give some due thanks to them.

In today's society people are pressured to 'generate knowledge', talking often, expressing themselves, self-styling, affirming: essentially advertising themselves and their identity long before the real accumulation of knowledge and reflection occur. At some level we can't begrudge this, and I'm really one to talk. Yet this is troubling considering people's moral motivations to commit violence. Most of us don't know precisely how to accumulate knowledge. People feel they must express themselves first, instead. This is, likely, worse than it used to be, due to technological, cultural, and social developments. It results in the proliferation of diffuse ideas and ideologies or a greater, dissociated scale of ideas and action that will be much more difficult to regulate or ever control using previous methods. The implications are anti-democratic—further democratic degradation, despotism, more conflict and violence.

Experts deal with this about as well as the public, which means not very well at all. They are pressured, consciously or implicitly, to speak grandly on things they know little or nothing about. Staying in one's lane becomes difficult, when it is sometimes advantageous to actually do that and not fear the limitations of one's knowledge or deferring to others. When experts, and not just the public, feel such a need—an almost righteous, narcissistic or otherwise arrogant compulsion—to comment about what they don't know (always a common phenomenon, though not so exaggerated in the past), this has wide implications—many of which are worrying or detrimental.

Speaking of expertise in general, academic expertise, people with some real brilliance or quality, or at least a perceived intellectual weight—such experts are commonly invited to speak about anything on the basis that they are knowledgeable people. But their knowledge is limited to a specific area; they are not omniscient. And many speak embarrassingly about what they know less about. When invited to express an opinion, experts are valuable. Especially valuable when they really are intelligible and cogent on a particular subject—and speak with confidence. When asked a question one doesn't have a good answer to, or which one has no answer to, it is more important than many think to say one does not know something, and to defer one's expertise. When experts talk outside their realm of competence, and do so poorly, they obscure what they are genuinely knowledgeable about. It is much more difficult for others to recognise real expertise when an expert expresses obtuse opinions that have a diffusing and dissociating effect. This is more important than many think.

Expertise matters. Without it we have a crisis of trust and a real threat to democracy. Speaking with Bernard Williams, we might say that democracy is bound to the practical virtue of truthfulness. And associated with trustworthy institutions. There exists a great crisis of trust in institutions today, as the world grows and things move very quickly, resulting in the proliferation of conspiracy theories and, further, greater conflict and possible violence. This is, in part, a self-inflicted wound as institutions struggle with how to conceive of themselves in contemporary society, with the greatly increasing demands and contradictions of a developing modern society, and this struggle contributes to distrust, made worse by the social climate and other nefarious interventions.

Experts talking about anything they like within this climate are more dangerous than they may consciously imagine. We can, or should, have a wide tolerance for speech (even destructive speech), but the contention here is the responsibility of the expert we fail to consider, or for that matter its wider implications. Experts talking about anything and everything, when their realm of expertise is deep but narrow, renders their virtues less clear and makes them appear less trustworthy. With the result that experts generally are then perceived as less trustworthy. Our struggle to make sense of things is compounded not just by the irresponsible talk of experts idly pontificating outside their domains, but by societal and technological demands.

Wide talk is sometimes useful, but there is, in part, less real dialogue and collaboration when we are subjected to a narcissistic broad expertise. People struggle to understand when an expert is truly knowledgeable and how, or when, to defer to whom. Greater societal distrust is a crisis for democracy—a lack of intellectual humility has troubling implications.

These thoughts are partly abstract, but they indicate that we are dealing with a moral climate influenced by the practical, industrial, technological demands of society. Which means, moreover, that solutions to some of our worst problems are not easy, though perhaps they would have been easier to rectify or mitigate in the past—in, again, a different social, technological, and cultural climate.

Many of us, whether or not experts in some field, wish to apply generalised or abstract rules to the world, predicated on how we think actors and powers should behave rationally, or based on pre-conceived notions, with very broad demographic and logistical considerations—rather than considering very particular and individual ways that nations, societies, or leaders, behave depending on their local and regional history, or their acute idiosyncrasies. This is closer to a game with set rules, or a formula, a scheme, a plan, than it is to reality. One cannot routinely apply a general rule of politics that would function in one place—say, the USA, or Russia, viewing the nations at a low resolution from far above—rather than more intimately investigating local developments and history. This is a type of cultural narcissism, manifest in American foreign affairs (consider American leftists thinking nations are only reactive to American activity, and without their own domestic considerations and history) or typical of Europeans when viewing America (snobbery), a projection of their own values and ideas, deemed obvious and evident, that makes Europeans think things should work according to their own criteria and worldview, without a more intimate reflection.

Responsible experts in specific fields exist. And we do better if we act with a greater intellectual responsibility to know this. The world is uncertain and trust has become rarer and rarer. It should still exist, and untactful relativism is an easy tool in the arsenal of autocrats and dictators—just as strident propaganda is. But truth, as Democritus once said, is in the depths. It isn't easy and requires prudence and responsibility—both resources in short supply across the world. We fail if we don't consider how to navigate this world, and mitigate its dangers.

Hola, Zinedine

Buenas noches, ladies, gentlemen, distinguished club-mates, members of the press. Ready for your questions.

How do we move? We move over the pitch; through time; off the ball; within language.

Also between languages? Yes, via translation, the written habit of moving a set of words from one pattern, arrangement, line-up, to another. This can take time, to read, stop, look up, hone. Or, we move between languages by interpretation, which is a spoken and performed behaviour, more immediate, allowing for conversation and questioning to take place in a quick one-two. It's live action.

What about movement between those two halves of the field, between the spoken and the written? That goes both ways. Transporting from the written word into the spoken is reading out loud (a brilliant invention). Converting the spoken word into recorded text is transcribing.

Is there a further activity which combines or complicates the two divisions, scoring both on translation between languages and on transposition between modes of utterance? *Sí.* One can read the words in their original language as they appear on the page; that is, following the instruction that the written letters tell you to make with your mouth. H-o-m-e spells "home" and is said in a certain way, it makes this sound rather than another. Or, one can read words from the page and contemporaneously change them, speak these other different noises, though what you are conveying has the same sense. You can read the letters *"volver a casa"* and say out loud the sounds "come back home."

And moving the thought onto the page? That's just writing. *No hay nada más, sabes.*

¿Why am I presenting this in question and answer format? Because the occasion that got me considering these activities around translation is a press conference that took place on 11th March 2019, when the former player Zinedine Zidane was introduced, re-introduced in fact, as the manager of the Real Madrid men's football team (I call it football; I speak English. This is, too, the language I write in). He fielded questions from the press, in French and Spanish; said, as the main thrust, that he was happy to be back.

What's good about this presser, involving as it does a tight focus on my sporting and cultural hero, as, in tight jeans, he negotiates words, in Spanish? If you have to ask, you'll never know, I'm tempted to say. But that is my task here, to convey, pinpoint, explain. So I'll lace my boots, get cracking.

Pero ahora soy uno más, I'm just one of many

First, in practical terms. What's the format of the 2019 presser, how do I encounter it? I watch it all on a YouTube clip provided by Real Madrid Football Club. There's half an hour of audio-visual, from a couple of cameras and mics in the conference room. Over the top of this is simultaneous interpretation, spoken words, from a young fellow who sounds like he's from Barnet, north London. And after quite a while I realised that the video had an option for an automatic closed caption or CC transcription of Zidane's output—white type, Spanish words—on the screen.

In addition, Real Madrid put out an English-language press release about the conference, with the questions very much condensed and Zidane's answers just lightly edited. This account of his words differs somewhat from the video. The gist, the direction of travel is the same, but the phrasing divisions and particular words chosen, these aren't quite the same as in the YouTube. For example, the press release transcript has, "I'm fully aware of the club I'm joining. Nobody can take the excitement . . ." But the Barnet boy interpreting on the video speaks that as, "I know where I am. I know where I've come to. Life is full of ups and downs. I'm buzzing!" Which as a conveyance of enthusiasm is back of the net, meaning, good.

I also know what Zidane is saying because the (UK newspaper) the *Guardian*'s website on the evening offered a live-blog of this momentous (to the football world) event, with every few minutes a textual snippet of the latest pronunciamento, interspersed with links from other sources, pictures of Zidane's outfit, jokes emailed in by readers. It's collage-ist, in form. The *Guardian* also had a correspondent over in Madrid giving live summary, further think pieces.

I have a range of inputs, then, and each one offers a subtly different translation of his words. And I can add to these myself: I can look at his mouth in Spanish and write down the sounds, then take this transcript away and use various assistants (linesmen? VARS?) to translate it into English. I have my insiders, in the language, and other sources. Though they're of varying reliability: when I ask Google Translate it offers me the idea that Zidane loves Real Madrid football club so much that he wants to feel it deep inside him, which, though pleasingly filthy, is probably not exactly the sentiment he's trying to convey. Sometimes the interpreter speaks over him, the captions interject odd words as artifacts. They drown or muddle his voice. Or maybe he's just not speaking textbookly correct Spanish. The more explanatory inputs there are, the harder it is to hear Zidane's own voice (a lesson, perhaps, but one that I'm resolutely ignoring).

But I use my discretion, combine these various sources and tools, to derive my own interpretation. There's the non-verbal too, of course: his demeanour, his gestures, his almost-giggle as he answers about just how many titles he's won, how successful he's been, in the past at Madrid. I love it when he laughs. There's a point when he's asked if the team lacked hunger, and he replies no, the only thing they needed was a change. He shrugs and chuckles, "*No hay nada más, sabes*"—there's not much more to it, you know. Then he laughs again, almost blushes, when recounting what people say to him when they stop him in the street. "*Cosas mal, eh, no todo las cosas buenas*"—some nice things, some not so much. "*Un poco de todo,*" a bit of everything. His body as he hunches forwards round the podium and grips the side—you're reminded that he's a big man.

All these elements, figures: I weave through them, line them up together, zigzag through this web of language, the compound sources, to get to the end, the double end, the ZZ. So, multiple inputs, but one voice is the central thread, the reason for it all: Zidane's claim that though he left this very role only nine months ago, he's happy to be back. That's the basic. But expanding, tangenting off from this centre circle, there are a few words and ideas that recur, that caught my notice; my studs snagged on them. Specifically, about time and repetition, language, and, returning to Madrid.

***Tenemos tiempo para hablar,* we have time to talk**

The simultaneous interpreter does a sterling job. But he's listening and responding, marking carefully wherever Zidane goes, not concurrently reading out a prepared, parallel language text. So sometimes his words clash with whatever it is that Zidane is saying next; they're slightly out of register. There's a time lag, and the voices bunch or clot slightly, as Zidane talks with a dynamism, with bursts of energy in his delivery; he pauses, thinks, listens to a question. The English interpreter, too, has to take time to listen, then he follows behind with his English-words-version of the same thing that Zidane said a few seconds earlier; Zidane's already run past, over-paced him, taken the ball round. His word "*ahora*" comes from his lips and appears on the captions at the same time, but it's not til a moment later that the interpreter tracks back and catches up with "now."

There's another thing about time. Over several repetitions Zidane mentions that he's returned as manager because he got a phone call from the president of the club, one Florentino Pérez. The story is that Pérez rang, asked if he'd come back, Zidane was delighted to, all is harmony. The journalists seem a little sceptical about this, but we'll let them play on. What I noticed is that the English interpreter with his not-cut-glass accent pronounces Pérez's job title with a slight contraction of word, so that as he describes it, Zidane says that "the present" called me, "and I like the present." We are pitched into, or reminded that we live in, the world of the immediate, the live. Live even as I toggle back and back, ceaselessly into the past, re-watching with admittedly obsessive interest this cultural occasion, revisiting from a distance of more than four years. I suppose it's still a live event to the extent that I'm finding it, poring over it, studying and exegesis-ing it, all this while afterwards, still. And it says "LIVE" on the screen in big letters in the top right corner.

There's repetition and extra time built in to everything that's happening at the presser. A bit because he has already been the *entrenador* at Real Madrid for a couple of years, with lower roles prior to that. We've been here before, this is a replay. And a press conference in which a manager explains to the journos how he's looking forward to this Saturday's match and everything will be great? That's happened so often it's practically Noh drama, ritual, same old drill. But time also loops and swerves because watching now (in 2023) is to watch from the vantage point of knowing that there will be, it has already happened, a second time that he steps down, again (this actually in May 2021). So we're watching him start in a role (in 2019) that we know has in our timescale already finished. Also, and even without the benefit of hindsight, everyone there at the presser knows that these things don't last long, however much you profess lifelong allegiance to a club. Football is short (ars brevis, *sabes*) and no-one at this level of football, in these dynamics and scenarios, will probably be in place very long. That's fine, we just run with it for now. But it won't last.

***Cosas . . . vamos a cambiar,* everything's going to change**

The president (or present) called me. A journo asks Zidane, "What's the first thing that went through your mind when the call came?" Hands-spread shrug, shake of the head, "*De volver . . . y aquí estoy.*" To come back, and here I am. That's it: he's dead-stopped the question with a phrase of excellent simplicity but existential pertience: *aquí estoy*. The exchange involves thought, returning, presence. He's picking up the ball here from Descartes' *cogito ergo sum*, I think therefore I am. I think, return, and here I am. (Or possibly from Bugs Bunny.) I thought *volver* might refer to his balletic and beautiful way of twisting, vortexing, outrunning opponents on the pitch. But no, the word had wrong-footed me; it's actually to return home, come back, drop back and mark. Not to spin, snick back, cut over a defender, not an individual motion and axis verb, but one which describes relative position vis-a-vis a larger whole; he mentions coming home, *a casa*, several times. Home, here, to Madrid. I live here.

Home, and change, *el cambio*. The players needed it, the club needed it. He needed a change, it had been time for him to go. I like this repetition of *cambio*, given that I'm considering the whole presser and the broader event in the context of changing between, going across between states, motion. He talks about change, then in one instant he effects change: he shifts both language and subject, as a question comes in from a French not a Spanish journo, asking about what's changed over nine months. Zidane is asked about change, but what he replies is about language: "I'm glad you asked in French, so that I can explain again and make sure the Spanish understand one thing better." "*Je vais être clair*," I want to make it clear, he insists.

Tampoco me he ido muy lejos, I didn't go far

So time, repetition, change, return, *volver*. But the main reason, the top scorer for why I thought about this event over the past four years, was this: as I had remembered it, Zidane's address contained an interesting phrase. What have you been up to, these past nine months, asked someone. And Zidane replied, "I have been here in Madrid, doing my thing."

I like this, its combination of the local and specific with the expansive, imprecise slang. What does he mean by it, what does it mean? Madrid? Yes, he lives there with his wife. Doing my thing? Pleasantly vague, indicating, "the sort of stuff I do." The speaker has a field, behaviour, disposition towards something that he doesn't want to explain in this sentence. Or doesn't need to; obviously "my thing" for Zidane—one of the most famous players then managers in the world—is going to be footy. But he distinctly has not been doing this; since the end of May the previous year, when he resigned for the first time from this very position of Real Madrid manager, he has not been involved in the game.

Or could he mean the opposite? "Doing my thing" as a way of saying, private matters that are none of your business, not my public persona of football. That would imply, I've been not doing the thing that you all assume forms me; there's been nothing of that going on. So when asked what he's been doing, his answer might be taken as either nothing, nothing at all, or football (though they are very close). I'd read it as football, every time. Or is "my thing" just vague because the activities are vague? Pottering around. I had breakfast, went to the shops. Watered my flowers. Cultivated my garden, my green space. Ironed my jeans.

Anyway, I liked this phrase very much. It seemed to contain both mastery of an activity and an at-homeness in both the world and the neighbourhood, and in one's chosen sphere. A sense of quiet contentment, the confidence that you know what you like, you're good at it, you can just get on with it away from the cameras, stadium, microphones. A groundedness in a particular place, a facility with the activities that you use your own body to do. It locates him in a city, and he's not just placed there, inert; he's doing his things. He's embodying presence through action. Which is completely what being a legendarily good footballer is about, to my mind: you think, you are here, you take up and understand space and you move over the pitch. The way you control your body within these geographical boundaries—inside the lines—is the skill. Oh there is the ball, too, but that's *menos importante;* it's more about space and action. Being here, doing this. I have been here in Madrid, doing my thing. I took it as my motto, or the state to which to aspire. I'd like, me too, to be able to explain myself thus.

Of course, though, he doesn't actually say this. He's speaking Spanish, anyway. The words that come out of Zidane's mouth, or that seem to from the video, are, *"A Madrid, vivo a Madrid, hacer mis cosas"*—*vivo*, I live; *mis cosas*, my things; *hacer*, to do. I can see why that moves over to the English sentence as I received it. It's a clean pass, the words in Spanish having their equivalents in English, and as I look at it I can see the sentence at its start point and at its end point, see it makes sense for the meaning to travel over to how it lands as a concept in my mind.

And he doesn't speak in such a written, complete manner as I had remembered the English. He's extemporising, off the cuff; sentences and thoughts over-run. This is not because he's inarticulate, but this is how people speak in words, rather than when they're using the control of the written language. It's how people interpret, rather than translate, their own thoughts, internal monologue, into speech. Zidane's a beautiful mover: not just over the grass, or pivoting so his volleying boot follows the perfect curve that will lead into the goal. He also has this lovely way for moving or distributing ideas, sending them out all over the pitch, the conference room, the internet, all the media; then further out, further. His thoughts move out as words, into transcript, interpreted speech, reported speech. Written material, literary sources. Words that can be passed, manoeuvred, released.

Me preguntas pero . . . , you can ask me but that's not the question right now

This is a press conference about a manager returning to work with a sports team. Why, then, do I look at it in terms of language; what's dragging me in and enticing me to look at it in this way? I've studied this, Zidane's words, much more exhaustively than I watch his spin, turn, shoot, score on the grass of the pitch. And I watch those a lot. From body to voice, what prompts the move from interest in his physical excellence to this dissection of his speaking? Most football players I don't care what they are chatting about; you've got to let the feet do the talking. But Zidane's words? I can't say. He doesn't talk much, but when he does it's nice, it's *cosas buenas*. When they announce him onto the stage, the Spanish compere gives his name the Castilian Spanish pronunciation: *Thinedine Thidane*. Not a buzzing Z sound like I'd say, nor a hissing French TS. His name moves. His eyes flicker. He steps up.

There's something slipping about all over the pitch, all through this presser, something to do with how we talk and convey what we want another to understand. About how different sounds and meanings move all over, through, alongside the person. I'm chasing hard but I can't quite catch up with Zidane, with what he's doing about words. Maybe it's not even the particular words but his facility with and between them, the way he has control over switching around, cutting back, making the point, while he fields the questions about how he turns or moves, changes or remains.

Este gran club, que quiero mucho. This great club, that I love very much

I have been here in Madrid doing my thing, says Zidane, sort of. This is what I want: to be at home in the world, like he's at home in Madrid, at home in my body in the space, in the same way that Zidane is. In a beautifully repetitive and imperfect way, knowing when to talk and when to shrug; when to change and when to leave it all *lo mismo*, just the same. To have the perfect timing to pick up the call from the present. Zidane makes things very simple. "*La vida es así*, life's like that. I know where I am, I know where I've come to."

He steps up, adjusting his blazer buttons. He reaches down but there's no button left to fasten so he hitches his belt buckle instead. He switches language. He moves it all around. He fiddles for ten seconds with the two little microphones on adjustable stalks, which wave there in front of him like flowers on stems. *Bueno*, he says. He smiles.

Gracias a Mark Wingrave y Juan Tabarés

Thomas Walton

Unsavory Thoughts

What We Love About Writers Are Their Behavioral Disorders

In the 1960s Joan Didion carried a typewriter around with her when she flew to assignments, flew to vacation destinations, flew to visit friends. She carried it in cabs to the airport, lugged it to her gate, had it on her lap on the plane. She carried two legal pads and pens as well, but more importantly, she carried a typewriter. Why? "To start typing the day's notes."

There's something wildly excessive about this. Especially seen from the 21st century. I have a manual typewriter. I don't carry it anywhere. It's heavy. It's basically decorative. It's on a shelf by a few bottles of liquor, gifted liquor, liquor we will probably never drink: Maraschino liqueur, Metaxa, a mini bottle of amaro, Bailey's, that type of thing. I don't even remember where they came from, those bottles.

A standard portable typewriter weighs about fifteen pounds. Fifteen pounds! Didion lugged that thing around with her. Found her gate, or a table near her gate, opened the typewriter, inserted a piece of paper, and started typing. Right there in the airport.

Am I wrong to find this extravagant? Was everyone doing this? I'm sure she was on a deadline, but even so. Couldn't she have just written her notes and typed them up when she got home? It must've seemed efficient, sensible, to carry a typewriter. Perhaps it was. Perhaps there was no other way.

She was, of course, mostly writing for someone else. For *Vogue* or *Vanity Fair* or the *San Francisco Examiner*, but it still strikes me as compulsive. Perhaps all writers are compulsive. Of course they are. Why does this surprise me? Why am I only realizing that now?

Compulsion is defined as "an irresistible impulse to act, regardless of the rationality of the motivation."

Was the motivation for Didion as simple as having a deadline, or earning a paycheck? I doubt it. I mean, that was in play of course, but not to the extent that you would carry a typewriter on and off a plane.

What we love about artists and writers, as much as if not more than their work, are their behavioral disorders. I love Didion's journalism, the spare prose and provocative political asides. The unfinished, uncooked quality of her "essays." How they seem to end before they begin. I love her writing, but I love her more knowing she was once wandering around Colombia or El Salvador in huge sunglasses and a tailored skirt, carrying a purse, a cigarette, and a Remington typewriter that weighed as much (according to a quick google search) as a bowling ball, four bricks, or a bag of seven pineapples.

That image, to me, is as wonderful as anything she wrote.

Reading *1984* Is Torture

I read George Orwell's *1984* and it was torture. By torture I don't mean the actual torture in the book (of which there is much), but the torture of description. The modern human mind can no longer tolerate descriptive writing. What's the point? Where's the action? Where's the sex? (I did like the romantic interludes, Mr. Orwell, the sex scenes in the park and in the secret room above the antique store were not only sparingly described, but/and/also surprising and inspired!)

Furthermore, the highly descriptive writing is describing in minute particulars a highly disturbing dystopian cityscape. Uglier than any downtown Portland Oregon in January, human zombies strewn about like scattered clothes at a Goodwill donation center. The dystopian novel has saturated our times. At least it *had* saturated our times up until a few years ago, when our times became actually dystopian. In the few years preceding the pandemic it was all dystopian fiction all the time, and usually in the form of a graphic YA novel—that form that is meant for, let's be honest, those who'd rather be watching TV, those who don't want to read but want a story to be shown to them. Reading YA is not just passively allowing a text to present itself to you, it's a form of catatonic couch potato-ism that requires little more brain activity than scrolling through TikTok.

Maybe the dystopian phase has passed? I don't know, time will tell. Perhaps now we prefer a softball, politically appropriate personal essay? A confessional essay? An essay that allows the reader to become a voyeur. Is all the world a fetish? Or do we just endlessly fetishize the world? And if you're always saying the "right" thing, aren't you always saying nothing? A scream in a theatre full of screaming people isn't a scream you can hear.

Forgive me, I digress.

While reading *1984*, I was surprised at how bored I was. Maybe the fact that Orwell is

English should have tipped me off. Or maybe boredom is the inevitable outcome of all seminal works. If you don't read the original first, and instead read the thousands of imitations of that original, the original then comes across as hackneyed. Sad. I arrived seventy years too late.

George Orwell is a nom de plume, as I'm sure you know. Orwell's real name is Eric Arthur Blair. An odd choice, to forego Eric Arthur Blair in favor of George Orwell. Eric Arthur Blair has a certain flare, but George Orwell sounds like someone who eats at a Cracker Barrel on Saturday night. You can hardly pronounce the name George Orwell without biting the side of your mouth.

Lastly, the book is also torture because of all the, well, torture. It just goes on and on and on. It's torture to read! Orwell/Blair certainly drive their point home. I guess? What's the point exactly of torturing Winston for fifty pages, essentially one fifth of the book? Twenty pages of electric shock and a rat eating out Winston's eyeballs would surely be enough. Now, I love violence just as much as the next American cis-white man of trash (I should confess here that I don't mind eating at Cracker Barrel on Saturday night or any other night), but don't we understand the nature of brainwashing without the rat eating out Winston's eye sockets? Don't we both understand it and yet also inexplicably succumb to it? And if we do still succumb to brainwashing and totalitarian propagandas, have we really understood? We understand and we accept, thank you very much. Please yes, march out another Trump, another Bolsonaro, another Kim Jung Un, another Meloni, we are ready and willing (and helpless against it?) to partake in a little propaganda swilling.

Perhaps I'm wrong. Maybe fifty pages of torture were too few.

I read *1984* and it was torture. The most torturously frightening notion isn't even in the book: the fact that despite the book being a scathing satire of fascism, totalitarianism, and sycophancy, we seem incapable of enacting the wisdom that it offers, and leap with arms out and brains disengaged into the cynical movements that would grind our humanity into meal.

Perhaps his pen name should've been George, Oh Well.

Rilke as Healing Agent

I FIND IT BIZARRE that the New Age community has embraced Rilke. Why? Why have some of his lines been taken out of context and placed around images of waterfalls or clouds, then packaged as greeting cards or needlepoint wall-hangings? I can't help but think that Rilke would be nauseated by most people who find him "enlightening." They've certainly never read an entire poem. And if they have, you can't convince me that they've understood it. You can't convince me that they haven't just reduced it to whatever feel-good spiritual slogan they most recently heard in yoga class or luxuriating in a sound bath.

Rilke would have us tear ourselves out of the social and religious clichés that to him were soporific. For Rilke, to be asleep was the ultimate crime. And what is a cliché if not a suspension of the mind? A hammock for thinking, or lack thereof? Rilke is a storm seducing storms.

Perhaps it's the fault of his patron, Princess Marie von Thurn und Taxis-Hohenboke. Or rather, not her fault but the fault of the fact that Rilke seems to have one eye on flattering her, and one eye on the sky. You could read the entire *Duino Elegies* as an over-the-top, shamelessly ingratiating grant application. (You could, but you shouldn't.) It is this tone, I think, that those who frequent Theosophy bookstores with names like Far West Pathways find so inspiring.

When he famously asks, in the *Elegies'* opening lines, "Who, if I cried out, would hear me among the angelic orders?" I'm guessing he didn't think it would be the folks at the Aspen Food Co-op, or the teacher of Thursday evening's Pilates and World Peace class.

His books are now face-out beside Thich Nat Than, Chogyam Trungpa, and Bhagwan Shree Rajneesh in New Age bookstores across the Western world. Here's a calendar with his quotes. Here's a yoga deck with fifty-two cards, fifty-two positions, fifty-two Rilkean reductions. And here's an embroidered pillow with "Many a star was waiting for your eyes only," written beneath the image of a child and mother gazing longingly at each other.

It's enough to give you food poisoning. Please, if you would, leave Rilke alone.

And lest we forget, in a letter to the Duchess Aurelia Gallarati-Scotti written in the 1920s, Rilke praised Mussolini and described fascism as a "healing agent." Why have I never seen that pillow in Mystic Journey Books and Gems?

Kevin Boniface

Natural History

It was the morning after a particularly stormy night, the same night our neighbour torched his shed. I didn't know this neighbour very well, we worked different shifts so we rarely bumped into each other. He was recognisable though for his striking appearance: tall and thin with a long scar that ran from the top to the bottom of the left side of his face. Style wise, he favoured the hairdo and eyewear of Nick Knox of the Cramps combined with the threadbare knitwear and army issue boots of a badger baiting youth worker from the 1970s. He'd once sold me a car battery for a fiver. Anyway, that night's strong winds ensured his fire not only spread to next door's fence and wheelie bin but also badly scorched their new secondhand Austin Montego. It was specifically the damage to the Montego which prompted the noisy fist fight in the street below my bedroom window at 2am.

"Look at the state of my fucking car you stupid fucking twat!"

The fire was still smouldering as I walked past it at 7am. As on most mornings back then, I was on my way up to the moor at the end of Frederick Street to release another mouse from one of the humane traps into which I'd naively put so much faith and peanut butter. It was as I rounded the corner into William Street that I happened upon the small ziplock bag full of exotic looking feathers. A flash of green caught my eye amongst the wind tossed takeaway-styrene of another tangled litter trap. I crouched and reached out an arm between the rotten fencing and the last remaining asbestos panel of what was once one of those mid-century garages for an Austin 1100. At full stretch, holding on to a deformed hawthorn for balance, I managed to snag the bag between my index and middle fingers. I stuffed it into my pocket and continued on my way to the moor where I released the mouse as usual.

Back at home I turned the key in the nightlatch, shouldered open the door and watched as a dozen or so mice scattered across the kitchen floor for the cover of the battered skirting. I swept the table top for droppings and put the kettle on; I disinfected the table so often in the couple of years I lived in that house that by the time I left I'd worn away any trace of varnish. I reached for the vintage Ty-Phoo tea caddy from the high shelf and dropped a tea bag into a mug. I'd started storing all my mugs, bowls and pans upside down in the cupboards after I'd found droppings and sticky yellow piss stains in them. I also kept all my food in metal containers otherwise the mice would eat it before I did. I'd once found a mouse asleep in a double-boxed pack of Shreddies and from that point on I scoured the charity shops for all the old bread bins, biscuit tins and sweet jars I could lay my hands on. I sat at the table and drank my tea, making sure I coughed, sniffed and shuffled my chair regularly lest the mice got the impression I'd left the room and decided to reemerge. Remembering the bag of feathers, I pulled it out from the pocket of the jacket on the back of my chair and tipped out the contents onto the table: six complete and very beautiful iridescent hummingbird skins. Stunning greens, pinks, purples, yellows and blues. Labels attached to each specimen read *Property of Bradford Museums* in an old-fashioned typewriter typeface.

I laid out the skins in front of me while I finished my tea. I stroked and teased the feathers into place until they were neat and pristine. They were obviously old and very fragile but were in good condition. They were beautiful.

I'd thought about keeping the bird skins but a few days later I phoned directory enquiries for a contact number at the museum. Remarkably the person answering the phone knew immediately what I was talking about. She explained that on that stormy night, the night my neighbour set fire to his shed, she decided to take a box of bird skins home with her to try to identify them over the weekend. She said she had a hell of a commute. Her usual hour-long drive took her almost two and a half hours and had been a stressful experience. Twice she was diverted around fallen trees and at one point the car in front was hit by a child's trampoline.

"It just came out of nowhere!"

When she finally turned off the main road, the flames from the neighbour's shed fire were leaping over the wall and across the street.

"By that point I just didn't care, I just drove straight through it!" she said.

She eventually arrived at her home up by the moor at the end of Frederick Street but when she opened the boot of her car a squall had swept the box of bird skins out of her hands. She scrabbled around with a torch and located all but one bag of specimens.

And so it was that I set off again, past the scorched ground where the shed had been, to reunite the birds with the curator of Natural History who was impressed that I'd known they were hummingbirds. I left her to ponder the specifics and went back home to my mice.

"Natural History" is taken from Kevin Boniface's *Sports and Social*, Bluemoose Books, September 2023.

Paolo Pergola

The Comet Star

One Day, as if out of nowhere, a comet may appear. In fact, it's an event that's already happened many times throughout history. Typically, when a comet appears, some people are compelled to follow it. For example, let's say that a comet becomes visible somewhere on the horizon, say in mid-air. Someone, for example one who exports myrrh or recycles gold or incense, could be inclined to think that, if they set off, they could get under it. Their wives might try to dissuade them, but they feel very attracted by the comet and so they set off. There are various tricks a comet does, though, that can be misleading. For example, to a myrrh exporter, it might seem that the comet is going in the opposite direction to the tail, but no, the trail is simply due to the effect of the solar wind, go figure.

But a primitive human, or in this case the myrrh exporter (for simplicity let's call him the myrrhman), who is essentially still quite primitive, could not have known this. So, when the myrrhman, who thought he was being smart, set up his own strategy to anticipate the movement of the comet, setting off not towards the direction where the star was, but towards where the star was going according to his approximate calculations, well, he was very wrong. Of course, day after day he could correct his shot; if he saw the star, let's say in the north but with the tail towards the east, then he walked towards the northwest.

To sum up, the myrrhman looked for the comet in the sky and followed it, trying to anticipate its movement. His goal was to get right under the comet. However, being "under" the comet is a bit subjective, because the universe is not two-dimensional, there-fore being "under" or "over" something like a comet depends on your point of view. It's not like if you have a comet at the zenith which means "over" you, then if it falls it will fall on you. Or else you may think you're getting closer to the comet and you didn't take into account the parallax, which the myrrhman didn't even know existed. Who knows what the myrrhman believed. It is possible that to find oneself under the comet, one may have to walk as far as the North Pole. And a myrrhman, even one riding a fast camel, may have been travelling at ten, twenty miles an hour at most, while the comet has better things to do than just wait for him. Not to mention that if he was trying to anticipate the direction of the comet's movement based on its tail, then no way, I don't see how he would ever find himself under it. This whole thing sounds a lot like Achilles and the tortoise.

Except if, mistake after mistake, it may also be that they canceled each other out. On one hand, the myrrhman wrongly anticipated the movement of the star, on the other, the parallax existed without his knowledge. The end result may well have been that one morning he myrrhman woke up in a barn and found himself right under the comet. It's a plausible outcome. And then, out of happiness, he would have gone to drink away the few coins left in his bag joined by a couple of gentlemen he'd met in a tavern. They were loaded with money anyways, since one of them recycled gold and the other one incense. In the end, the three of them got quite drunk and returned to the myrrhman's barn only to find out that a family of newlyweds had occupied it along with a donkey and a cow. All they could do, then, was to sleep outdoors, though with the comet star directly over them.

Tomoé Hill

Scents of Grace

1.

There can surely be nothing of sanctity in that high white chemical scent, one of constantly disinfected floors and surfaces. The deliberate, human removal of the traces of other bodies. In these halls, they stave off its opposite, the earth and mould of inevitability, the terrible moss of forgetting. All is exposed and bare: surrounded by tubes which mimic veins and airways in sterile, transparent efficacy. Here, the body is not the body; all flesh submits to the indifference of its sustaining double.

2.

Where do you think you are? he hisses with an alarm she has never before heard, nor will after. *Hide that.* She slides the silver and wood rosary beneath her sweater, instead wears her guilt openly. Trailing him down the corridor, she is shocked at his shock. In this place, does he harbour his own guilt over never introducing her to god, God, gods, or is it that in wearing the beads she gives away her unknowing? She young enough to be ignorantly, unconsciously faithful; faithless in good faith, interpreting the scent of tarnished silver in her mouth as a sign.

3.

The name of the saint the hospital bears has no meaning for her but she remembers the time she went, out of curiosity, to a local church summer school. They told the story of Moses, and she kept asking why about something—the answer to which, like an echo, was faith. There was something inside of her that could not stop at this word, pushed against the gentle suggestion to take the word inside herself as the world. But like a ball thrown repeatedly at a wall, she found this word coming back. At night, in bed, she would ask herself what she believed in, with only a vague awareness of belief as a thing which would never leave her.

4.

Walking back home from the church along an alley, pale orange Angel's Trumpets cascade over a fence, starting to bloom but withholding their sweet poison announcements until night. Not knowing why, she runs back to the church yard, not to find comfort within, but without; the solitary ginkgo tree which her mother greets as a friend each time they pass by. She plucks a ridged, fan-shaped leaf, then, returning home once more, waves it towards the flowers which curl with imagined malice in her direction, a gesture of defiance at an undelivered message.

5.

There were years when she cried upon smelling Paco Rabanne Calandre but could not understand why. Much later in the clash of memory and dream which reveal our innermost repressions like triumphant cards, it came back to her. It was the scent of those perpetual dream-halls in lux aeterna: walking through doors with the wind blowing you both towards and away from death, the metal grilles of hospital beds which moved silent passengers to their various destinations.

6.

He died untouched: that rare innocence represented a kind of saintliness, a holy fruit she left to rot in her own unconscious behaviours. He, high and white, she, low and dark. The stinging aldehydes of industrially clean sheets like Estee Lauder White Linen versus the syrupy fermentations of bottles and bodies in something like Dior Santal Noir, but neither of which signalled to the ideas of Heaven or Hell. Rot recalls the ginkgo again, when it changes with the season and its nuts emit a rancio scent of sweet rich decay. How when she found that scent in the taste of certain sherries as an adult, she thought of her mother under the golden tree and her own warding off of the Angel's Trumpets.

7.

At other times, she likened them to anaerobic and aerobic but could never decide which applied to her in her now-closed-off life. Then there is the question of bacteria, as she cannot shake certain associations, things left to the light without air that breed with vicious intent, the curious opposing scents of black mould and green: one musty and dry, the other thick and luxuriant. She wonders if all this time she has continued to grow only for the purpose of someday being unleashed like a vengeful plague upon herself.

8.

She knew J.-K. Huysmans meant only a state of grace when he spoke of saints dying 'in the odour of sanctity', but she undertook an olfactory exhumation nevertheless. The moss of forgetting now torn away in a desperate attempt to recall a body that once was. They had been children, barely with their own scents: hers yet to develop, so replaced with artifice, his new and never to be combined with another's to form a memory; wasted skin becomes wasted skin. Has her life been an attempt at resurrecting his through her own?

9.

There were entire patches of yard so untouched by sun that no grass ever grew. They would sometimes sit there under the tree or evergreen bushes hidden in the perpetual scent of fall, doing nothing but plucking at the bark or moss or mushrooms in the way blood and love need no excess conversation. They would look out at the yard of the house in which their fathers had grown up, never thinking of who would first lie beneath and who would remain above. What faith there was in the scents of your fathers being your own, unchanging.

10.

It is only ever lilies, violets, or aldehydes that she can still conceive saints smelling of in their last breaths; the high and powdered ethereal, a gossamer life dissolving into the next, burning the sinuses of those left behind. Roses seem too brash, despite knowing there is a particular saint associated with them. Tuberose feels the opposite of saintly, a flower of possessed flesh. Anyone with such knowledge senses it in Bernini's sculpture of the angel with Saint Teresa; feels its carnal throbbing within her to-be-pierced marble breast, the arrow which unleashes the senses.

Carnation? Perhaps, though the prickle of clove in its depths would seem to be an unwanted temptation, a fire smouldering in the depths. Aldehydes remain the most fitting in their way: clean, sharp, amplifying, effervescent, an eternal upwards trajectory towards the divine. Then, she wore a cheap gardenia or lily of the valley—Alyssa Ashley French Garden Flowers, on the cusp of ascent or descent, depending on how you choose to interpret her skin's desires.

Secretly, she has asked herself if turning away from the more pure and delicate florals has been a deliberate rejection of innocence. Examining her collections, everything indicates escape, carnality, luxuriance, the dream. But looking closer, there are still reminders. The summer ivy and cypress of Goutal Bois d'Hadrien, the cool evergreen and caramelised smoky woods of Chanel Sycomore and Miller Harris Vetiver Insolent, the dark heart of a childhood garden before the light intervened.

Kurt Luchs

Ah, Did You Once See Borges Plain?

Jorge Luis Borges needs no introduction, I think to myself. Then I think again, recalling that we are living through a new dark age when much of the past, including the literary past, is being discarded wholesale in a kind of cultural amnesia or cultural lobotomy. And I think perhaps I had better introduce him anyway.

He was born in 1899 in Buenos Aires, Argentina, and died in Geneva, Switzerland, in 1986 at the age of 86. Among other things we can say about the young Borges, he would have instantly recognized the reference to a line by Browning in the title of this essay. He was raised to be bilingual, speaking only English until age four. His knowledge of English and American literature was encyclopedic, surpassing any other Latin American writer of his generation. No doubt this was instrumental in his eventual choice of profession: librarian. Has anyone ever written so often or so imaginatively of libraries and librarians?

Borges started writing as a child and never stopped, perhaps influenced by his father, Jorge Guillermo Borges Haslam, a successful lawyer and teacher, but a failed writer. As the son would later experience, the father also had deteriorating eyesight, and moved the family to Geneva, Switzerland, in 1914 so he could receive medical treatment. They remained abroad until 1921, after spending a few years in Spain. It was there that Borges affiliated briefly with the avant-garde Ultraist movement, which was a reaction against Modernismo.

Back in Buenos Aires, he wrote furiously, publishing his first book of poetry in 1923, *Fervor de Buenos Aires* (*Fervor of Buenos Aires*), and his second in 1925, *Luna de enfrente* (usually translated as *Moon Across the Way*, though in person I heard him call it *The Moon Across the Street*). In 1925 there also came his first book of essays, *Inquisiciones*, (*Inquiries*). He made important longtime friends, such as Victoria Ocampo, founder of *Sur* magazine, the country's leading literary organ, and Adolfo Bioy Casares, who would become his close collaborator. Although poetry was his first love, and he never gave it up, he devoted more time to the short prose hybrid forms on which much of his fame is justly based. Borges is almost certainly the most influential fiction writer who never completed a novel. He inspired not only generations of writers in his own language, but also in English and many others.

The other significant thing that happened during those early years was the gradual onset of his blindness. In 1928 he had the first of eight eye operations. Within 25 years he was completely blind. This tragedy affected every aspect of his existence. Yet he managed to find some blessings in it. One of his later books of poetry is called *Elogio de la sombra* (1969) (*In Praise of Darkness*). Of necessity, blindness sharpened his hearing and his memory, two gifts that made him a better poet.

Before I embark on an analysis of his tiny poem "A Minor Poet," I need to recount two of my own memories. The first is of a visit Borges made to Northwestern University in Chicago. I think it was 1974. He had been famous in America for two decades by that time. The place was packed. Borges spoke for a bit about his love for English and American literature, and how that love influenced his own work. He recited some favorite poems from memory, along with a few of his own. Then he took questions.

Someone who knew his work well asked what a particular line in one of the poems from his second book was about. I wish I could remember which line and which poem! Anyway, that's when he referred to the book as *The Moon Across the Street*. He was somewhat dismissive of his early work. "Honestly, I don't know what I meant," he admitted. "Probably I was just trying to come up with the most startling image possible. That's what I did in those days."

Another person asked who were his favorite American poets. Not surprisingly, he mentioned Whitman and Dickens and Frost. But there was an audible gasp of surprise and embarrassment when he said he loved Carl Sandburg, then very much out of favor with the literati. Maybe he still is, I don't know. Borges quoted "Fog," the one we were all taught as schoolchildren, and I believe he mentioned "Chicago" and "Washington Monument by Night," two more great American poems, no matter what trivial fads and shunnings may occur in our little literary pond. Sandburg's love for his native city must have resonated with the man who had a lifelong love affair with his own Buenos Aires.

I asked a question as well, which is the subject of one of my two tribute poems accompanying this essay, the one called "What Borges Said" (the other is called "Another Minor Poet"). It was an idiotic question— what did he think of the horror and science fiction author H. P. Lovecraft? Still, he answered it in a way that made me feel slightly less idiotic while casually revealing the depth of his knowledge. How many American poets alive then could have done that? Precious few.

My question was perhaps the second stupidest one that day. I am pleased to report that the most imbecilic question was asked by another preening windbag. This nitwit wanted to know if Borges would comment on Thomas Pynchon's *Gravity's Rainbow* and what he called "the gravity of comedy." That sprawling novel had just been published the year before. Today many critics regard it as one of the finest American novels. That's as may be. Yet how fatuous to assume that Borges would have had any chance to read it. I doubt very much whether there was an audio or Braille version at that time. The only way Borges could have known the book is if he had had someone read it aloud to him, all 760 densely-packed, surreal and paranoid pages.

After the event, I had a chance to say hello and thank you to Borges. Just that, not even my name. But that was enough.

Fast-forward 38 years to 2012. Life, divorce and the vagaries of my so-called career had exiled me to Lewiston, Idaho, away from my children and any trace of human civilization. It was the worst two years of my life. Except, there was a good university nearby in Moscow, Idaho, and also a top-notch independent bookstore, BookPeople. One night they had a special event featuring Willis Barnstone, an excellent poet and easily one of the two or three best translators in the English language. Right now I'm looking at a copy of his first published work, *80 Poems of Antonio Machado*, from 1959. Good luck finding that anywhere at any price, though I will gladly let you come to my house and read it while I sit nearby with a loaded revolver.

I said hello to Barnstone and thanked him for his many translations, singling out those he had done of Borges. That got him reminiscing and talking. We spent the next hour on a couch discussing Borges in general and that visit to Northwestern University in particular. It turned out Barnstone had been one of his assistants and handlers on that lecture tour. I had already met him, in fact, all those years ago. He was 47 on that day in 1974 and 85 as we sat in BookPeople chatting about it, and it was as if not a moment had passed. He remembered every detail of the talk by Borges and also the questions, including mine and the one from the fan of *Gravity's Rainbow*.

Meanwhile, I was shamelessly monopolizing him, and the other attendees were getting increasingly annoyed and restless. I reluctantly released Barnstone back into the wild, deeply moved by this unexpected encounter. Something had been reawakened in me: the love of poetry. Not just reading it, but trying to write it again. A couple of years later I abandoned humor writing after several decades with the *Onion* and stints writing for television and radio. I returned to my first love, poetry. And in part I have to thank Jorge Luis Borges and Willis Barnstone for realigning my chakras, or whatever that was on those two mysteriously connected occasions.

As you can see, this essay is very personal for me. They say you should never meet your heroes. However, I met one of mine in 1974—two, actually—and they did not disappoint.

The Borges poem we'll be looking at here is one of his shortest, only two lines and eight words (nine in the original Spanish), or 11 words counting the title, "A Minor Poet." It should not be confused with an earlier poem bearing a similar title and theme, "To a Minor Poet of the Greek Anthology," which has been beautifully rendered in English by W. S. Merwin. This later, much more concise poem was first included in the book *The Gold of the Tigers: Selected Later Poems* (1977), translated by Alastair Reid. Technically, it is part of a set of otherwise unrelated brief poems gathered under the title "Fifteen Coins." I believe this means we are allowed to quote it in full here, as it was originally part of another longer poem.

Regardless of how it was first presented to the world, it stands on its own:

A Minor Poet

The goal is oblivion.
I have arrived early.

In case you were wondering, it is just as simple and unadorned in the original Spanish as it is in English. It does not rhyme. It is too short to establish any other distinctive sound patterns involving alliteration or assonance. Nor does it feature any "startling images" like those that festooned his earliest poems, the ones I heard him speak of almost with contempt or regret. It was said that later he bought up any copies he could find of some of them, simply so that he could destroy them and return them to oblivion.

No, this little poem depends almost entirely upon the most direct, straightforward kind of statement. Yet so much is contained in it, I feel. The key word, I believe, is "goal." "The goal is oblivion." Not, "The result is oblivion," or "The thing that happens is oblivion," or "The destination is oblivion." The *goal*. Whose goal, though? Surely not the poet's. God's goal, maybe? The goal of the universe, or existence? How strange, if the goal of existence is nonexistence, as if existence is some sort of aberration. And why oblivion instead of, say, death or darkness or silence? Oblivion, total erasure, seems more final than any of those I suppose. These un-spoken and unanswered questions linger in the mind long after reading the poem.

The second and last line—what would be the punchline if this were a joke (and perhaps it is in a way)—is a real heartbreaker: "I have arrived early." Of course, part of being a minor poet, the fate of nearly all of us, is that we never arrived anywhere at all. We tried, we gave it our best shot, we may even have written a few lines or a few poems worth remembering. Only they will not be remembered. Nor will we. Oh, oblivion, yes, there's a goal we all can meet! Some sooner than others, that's all.

We can think of this poem almost as one of those tantalizing fragments by Sappho (Willis Barnstone translated her too, check it out), pieces of lost poems so intense that even in partial form they remain poems in their own right. It's nearly a fractal of the earlier, longer poem (which is also a great poem), and yet it contains all that matters from that poem. It has not quite reached the goal of oblivion, though it is getting awfully close. Ironically, by writing it along with so many other memorable verses, Borges will not be arriving early at oblivion. Make no mistake, however, he will arrive at the place that receives us all, minor poets and major alike. And there may be worse things than oblivion. You could be the poor hapless fool who asked that silly question about *Gravity's Rainbow*. To quote yet another minor poet, "So long lives this, and this gives life to thee."

TIMING LESS PROBLEMATIC THAN TWO-TIMING.

Two After Borges

What Borges Said

Argentina's greatest export, the maker
of fables disguised as essays
and poems disguised as translations,
was on a lecture tour
of the United States, already blind,
led around by Willis Barnstone
and other good friends.
I saw him at Northwestern University
but he never saw me,
and when my turn came
to ask him a question
all reason left me and I blurted out,
"What do you think of H. P. Lovecraft?"
He smiled and said,
"Wonderful imagination.
Terrible writer. But when a man
has a name like Lovecraft
he has already given us everything.
We need ask nothing more of him."

Another Minor Poet

(after "A Minor Poet" by Jorge Luis Borges)

The song I hope to sing is one
where the words march into the whiteness of the page
like Captain Robert Falcon Scott trudging toward the South Pole,
fated to arrive five weeks after Amundsen,
that damned Norwegian upstart, and even worse,
doomed to die on the return journey,
braving the vast Antarctic icebox again at forty below.

There is no shame in being the second man
to reach the Pole or walk on the Moon (who was that again?),
no dishonor in being the first forgotten,
snow-blind, descending into darkness by means of the light.
The sweet amnesia of snow and cold is no less merciful
than that of the poem never written, never published,
or perhaps, published and quickly lost among so many others.
Though we appear to be hurtling away from each other
we are all on the same journey,
unknowingly following imaginary, invisible longitudinal lines
that must meet in the long night at the wrong end of Earth.

Henrietta Goodman

GG Allin Made Me Write This

My son is researching the Pocket Pussy. I thought the device was mostly a joke, but the industry is huge, especially a brand called the Fleshlight, which looks like a large flashlight until you take off the cap and find a rubbery-looking pink or tan or brown vagina or asshole or mouth at the opening of a tube lined with various battery-operated rings and protuberances.

Semen tastes like light. I don't tell my son this as he's showing me the Fleshlights modeled after the genitalia of porn stars, each with a license for their own "brand." The selection process starts with pictures of the women—you click one to read about her, then click *choose orifice*. The choices are *lady* or *butt*. I've told a few men about the light thing, and they've each taken it as an individual compliment, rather than an observation about all semen—a synesthetic feeling at the back of the throat that's less taste than brightness.

My son narrows his choice to four Fleshlights, shows me the corresponding porn stars and asks *which one do you think I should get?* He means which porn star and which body part, and because I especially don't want to think of my son in connection with the disembodied asshole of a porn star, I say *probably the vagina?* One of the porn stars is from Prague, so we pause for a geography lesson. In the description of her Fleshlight, which he reads aloud, he learns the words *interspersed* and *evocative*. It's more than he learned in the last trimester of 10th grade, online-pandemic version, which ended a few weeks ago.

But we did learn to knit a hat, since one of his classes was Pandemic Fiber Arts. His teacher posted links to YouTube videos and gave simple assignments like *Watch these videos and knit a hat.* As if everyone had a quarantined grandma at home baking cookies and waiting to gather the grandkids on her lap with yarn and needles. I didn't know how to knit. We slowed the videos down until the sweet plump women sounded gutter-drunk and then sometimes my son said *fuck this* and threw the needles on the table and went to his room and I sat there repeating *fuck this* and trying to cast on. Until we finally got it, and we knitted a pink hat and got an A.

My first husband took his second wife to Prague on their honeymoon and came back unable to shut up about how great it was in Pra-ha, as they call it in Prague and as they don't call it here, unless they are Czech or extremely pretentious. I was so glad I didn't have to go with him to Pra-ha or some mosquito-infested Blue Ribbon trout stream or the home of his evangelical Christian parents ever again.

The summer I was sixteen, in 1987, I could have gone to see GG Allin in Charlotte at the Church of Musical Awareness, an all-ages punk club across the street from The World-Famous Milestone Club, where I spent almost every weekend night of my whole four years of college. But I didn't go, because the Church had shitty bands, and my friends and I had only a vague sense of who GG Allin was, and we were unimpressed.

My first husband is the author of one sentimental novel that includes a sex scene—the kind that makes you feel embarrassed for the writer who didn't have the good sense to be embarrassed for himself. There's a *strong female protagonist* who is rescued again and again by the *even stronger male savior*, who is also the love interest. It's set in the Great American West and has a happy ending.

Maybe he should have read some Holub in Pra-ha.

Miroslav Holub wanted privacy, anonymity. As a personal self, he's not usually present in his poems, nor is he sentimental. He mostly separated himself from his work, à la "Tradition and the Individual Talent," creating poems that were clinical, intellectual, sometimes ironic and funny. His "Napoleon," for example, describes schoolchildren who know nothing about Napoleon Bonaparte but feel sad for a dog named Napoleon who's abused by a mean butcher. Nowhere in this poem does Holub appear, nor is the reader subjected to a sex scene. The poem is not about the Napoleon complex. Although Czech scholars Jiri Holy and Jan Culik find the poem to be an "homage to personal experience . . . which always eventually prevails over theory, ideology or interpretations of history," it's nonetheless also a poem about ignorance.

If you Google *was Napoleon good or bad?* you might be relieved to see that others have Googled it also, and that the answer is not simple. American History was only class in history or politics I was required to take in high school. The teacher was short and fat with a red nose—a drinker. All we did was play Trivial Pursuit, a game I was not good at. Sometimes it feels too late to catch up. I'm doing better with the U.S., but Syria? Ancient Rome? Yemen? It's easier to stay rooted in the personal, domestic present. Out in the street a neighbor calls *Bootsie, Bootsie*, and I really hope Bootsie comes home.

Lately I socialize with my son and our cats and the neighborhood cats, though not Bootsie, whom I've never met. The cats don't know or care about the gaps in my education, but my son at least knows I believe ignorance might be easier, but not better. Mystery Cat, who's gray and feral, cries at the back door at 3 a.m. and runs away when I open it. But I put out food anyway. He's hungry. He's scared. He doesn't know I would never hurt him.

There's a surprisingly large amount of video footage of GG Allin: grainy recordings of live shows, interviews and other material from several documentaries, like the party scene in which a young woman grants his birthday wish by peeing in his mouth. The comments on the videos are extensive, most left by people who are there to scoff but who are, nonetheless, there. A few are left by genuine fans, or the curious, and those who aren't totally dismissive make many attempts to retroactively diagnose him, as when, two years ago, someone named Stacey Smith wrote: *I see a sad guy who had schizophrenia and a massive drug problem. He had an abnormally abusive child hood, and I'm really surprised he made it that long . . .* Forty replies follow, some of which argue that he wasn't schizophrenic but had various personality disorders or was bipolar *for sure*. Others describe him as a *typical junkie*, followed by disagreement as to what a *typical junkie* would or wouldn't do. Then there are those who argue, like Tha3rdworldghost, that *he was sane and well aware of his actions*, or Star Pillars, who writes: *he was also a massive troll . . . he really liked to trigger certain people just for fun, and much of it was exaggerated as well as stage performance.* The other 2,349 comments, many of which have as many replies as the Stacy Smith thread, contain discussions about what it means to be punk rock, what is or isn't performance art, what his childhood was like, whether there's a double standard regarding a man who's covered with shit versus a woman who's covered with shit, and one very long, possibly serious, well-written speculation that Allin was *assassinated* for being *a misunderstood militant Buddhist*.

About the Czech Republic, I know only a little. I know Vaclav Havel was a writer and a Velvet Underground fan, and the word *Velvet* in *Velvet Revolution* had to do both with the revolution's lack of violence and with Lou Reed and Andy Warhol. My son learned who Warhol was because last year I bleached his hair nearly white and he looked like the puffball of a dandelion, and I told him he looked like Andy Warhol and he said *who?* so I showed him the Campbell's soup cans and Marilyn Monroe and a picture of Warhol and he said *yeah I kind of look like him.*

I am not embarrassed for GG Allin.

After the Pocket Pussy research, my son is so bored he asks if I want to play the Professor Noggins card games I bought when he was nine or ten, which have been stacked on the bottom of his bookshelf collecting dust: *Outer Space, Explorers, Prehistoric Mammals, The Human Body.* We pick *The Human Body*, and turns out we don't know much more than we did five years ago, but this time we learn about the hyoid bone, the only bone in the human body that's not connected to any other bone. It's under the tongue. It helps people speak.

When my son was very small, he used to collect all the clips and bands and bobby pins and put them into my hair while I sat on the couch pretending to be in a fancy salon and trying not to say *ow*. At the end, he'd bring me a mirror and I'd *ooh* and *ahh* over my "hairstyle." In the past couple of years, I've bleached my son's hair, dyed it black, streaked it blue, purple, red, and pink, and split it down the middle, white on one side, black on the other. I'm not very good at it, but he's happy with the results and goes off to school to be made fun of as though weirdness is both hereditary and a matter of pride.

The track list from GG Allin's 1989 album *The Suicide Sessions:*

1. Dagger in my Heart
2. Shit on my Prick
3. Cornhole Lust
4. Spread Your Legs, Part Your Lips
5. I Live to Be Hated
6. Stick a Cross Up a Nun's Cunt
7. Jailed Again
8. I Want to Burn
9. Lillian Phone Fucker
10. Pain & Suffering
11. Troubled Troubadour of Tomorrow
12. Liquor Slicked Highway
13. Can't Afford the Bail
14. Drug Whore
15. I Will Not Act Civilized
16. I'm Dying, I'm Dying, I'm Dead

Without my son and the cats, I'd be the human equivalent of the poor unattached hyoid bone, so I try to watch pretty much every video my son wants to show me, even the ones of Trump supporters saying endless stupid shit, or people dancing with no sense of rhythm and no trace of embarrassment so you can't tell whether they're serious, or the one he's shown me 17,000 times of RiffRaff wearing grills that make it look like he has gaps between his teeth like the Wife of Bath or a little kid with bottle rot saying *my main goal is to blow up and then act like I don't know nobody, hahahahaha*. I won't watch people being pranked or getting hurt, like the one in which a guy and girl are arm wrestling and her arm visibly, audibly snaps. Once he showed me a really cute video of otters, and I kept waiting for something bad to happen and nothing did—he just wanted to show me cute otters. For years, he wouldn't share what he listened to with me. I thought he didn't even like music. Then he started saying *want to hear my favorite song?* and showing me an elderly white person rapping, or Lil B's "Ellen Degeneres" song. Then he started showing me what he actually likes: Lil Wayne. Lil Peep. Lil Tracy. Dylan Ross. He shows me Nardwuar interviews, and now I watch them on my own because Nardwuar is even older than I am and deliberately nerdy and knows everything about everyone and will never not be cool.

After the Human Body game, my son shows me a video of Nardwuar giving Lil Uzi Vert a bobblehead of GG Allin with a little pile of poop at his feet, and another one, two years later, of Nardwuar again with Lil Uzi Vert, giving him a bust of Allin as a zombie with worms threading his flesh. In the first one, Lil Uzi Vert, wearing glasses and short purple dreads, seems happy and a little high; in the second, he claims to be Allin reincarnated, then stops and asks *where am I?* then *is ecstasy legal here?* In another video, when the interviewer asks why he likes Allin, all he can do is repeat *He was crazy, man . . .* My son has never heard of GG Allin, which is how all this begins.

In one of the videos showing how the Fleshlight molds are made, a porn actress named Riley Steele has her mouth and ass molded. The process involves a lot of pinkish rubbery slime being piled on, covered with thick white gauze as it hardens, then peeled off. At the end of the video, Riley, who's blonde and peppy as a cheerleader, says in a childishly flirtatious voice: *thanks for coming with me to do my new Fleshlight molds of my mouth and my little butthole! Now, you can fuck it! It'll be on the market soon, and you better fuck it!* Then she blows a kiss.

Most people say GG Allin had no talent, and it's true that his songs are neither complex nor particularly memorable, the lyrics often repulsive. But his voice, when he wasn't just screaming, wasn't bad. His covers of Warren Zevon's "Carmelita" and Patsy Cline's "Pick Me Up on Your Way Down," from his "outlaw country" album *Carnival of Excess*, sound a little like Deer Tick's John McCauley. His own songs on the album, like "Outskirts of Life," are kind of catchy, like a less sanitized version of Social Distortion: *Within the perimeters of this world I just don't feel*

real right . . . I'm living by myself on the outskirts of life . . . And his earlier "When I Die" is a straight-up country song with lyrics that describe, in unsettling detail, his funeral:

> *When I die put that bottle in my hand*
> *All these years on earth, it was my only friend*
> *When you dig a hole and gonna bury me*
> *Put that bottle of Jim Beam to rest beside me . . .*

Most of his songs are an extension of his stage persona—the lyrics unintelligible in live performance but graphically disgusting on the page. There's a difference between those songs and some of the country ones, which, in their assertions of alienation, self-reliance, and the inevitability of death, contain a resolute anger that seems truer to the person Allin might actually have been than all the theatrics. But what do I know? He didn't make or ask for a distinction between self and art (are we calling it art now?). If he had written poems, he would have found the idea of "the speaker" laughable. In her review of his collection of prison journals, letters, and drawings published as *My Prison Walls* in 2013, Margarita Shalina writes: *Considering GG Allin appeared to be a whirlwind of chaos on stage . . . , it is revealing that he is astutely aware of being his own product like every other artist, writer, musician, and performer. In a sense, this legitimizes his art.* Yes, we are calling it art now.

Even a song like "Watch Me Kill" (*I beat her more and more, I beat her 'till the blood gushed out, then I raped that bleeding whore . . .*) is perhaps not quite as simply stupid and gross as it appears, since it's a rewrite of the Appalachian murder ballad "The Knoxville Girl," which has been recorded by at least 28 different artists since 1924 and was derived from an Elizabethan ballad, "The Cruel Miller," written around 450 years ago. So maybe the question is not, *why would anyone want to listen to this horrible song written by a man who hated women?*, but *what the fuck is wrong with cultures that consistently, over centuries, produce song after song about men murdering women?* Of course there are songs about women killing men, too. You could make a really cool mix-tape.

When I was a teenager, my mother hated the music I listened to. She had gone to London on a Fulbright in the mid-1950s to study the clarinet, and the most contemporary music she appreciated was Benny Goodman, whom I loathed even more because we shared a last name. So I was in my room, being not the hyoid bone not because I was connected to my mom, but because I was connected to bands like The Replacements, my favorite, whom I discovered when I was thirteen on a late-night radio show called Flipsides that aired from Davidson College. I still have tapes of a few of the shows, recorded through the static of my bedside clock-radio—some college DJ from 1985 saying happily: *Confusion in the record booth! Spinning the disks!* Whenever I tried to share a song I liked with my mother, she scoffed at the repetitive simplicity of the music, the idiocy of the lyrics. It was like she couldn't even hear it.

Does it take talent to get up in front of a crowd of students at New York University in the florescent-lit student center, to stand there utterly naked and mush a peeled banana up your ass? That's what GG Allin does in the 1993 documentary *Hated: GG Allin and the Murder Junkies* after director Todd Phillips sets up the performance. Maybe it doesn't take talent, but it takes something, and I don't think the something can be reduced to mental illness. I don't want to do it myself, and I don't particularly want to watch it, but on the other hand, who wouldn't look out at all those smirking comfortable faces and not want to shove something up someone's ass?

Twenty years ago, one of my students in a freshman composition class wrote an essay about being a teenager, lying on his bed one afternoon with his mom listening to Nirvana when *Nevermind* was first released. He described the music as a revelation, an experience spiritual in its intensity, and shared. It was a lovely essay, and I was so envious.

Much Internet debate centers around the question of whether GG Allin was a rapist. In late 1989 to early 1991, he spent fifteen months in prison, convicted of assault following an incident with a woman that apparently began as consensual but did not end so. Aside from that, despite his claims of regularly raping women and men at his shows, those acts don't seem to fit the definition of rape. As Shalina writes, *It's hard to believe that anyone attended a GG Allin show accidentally.* He took laxatives for the purpose of shitting onstage. So, you might get shit on. You might get hit. You might get your face shoved into his crotch. There are videos of these things happening, but the people they happen to don't seem to mind. You could avoid these things by not going to the show, or maybe just by standing as far from the stage as you could get.

Ten years ago when I was getting my PhD I took a nonfiction workshop from a professor who talked about how important it is to be *professional* in one's decorum and appearance when giving a reading. For instance, she said, a poet had given a reading on campus the year before wearing fishnet stockings and boots, and *THAT* was *NOT* what one should wear. *Jill,* I said, *that was me.* My fellow students stared. Some of them surely remembered the reading from fall semester of the previous year. Though in her version I was dressed like a 1980s prostitute, in actuality I had worn, yes, fishnet tights, not with a micro-mini but a simple A-line skirt and a pair of well-worn harness boots. I was 38, with two decades of experience giving readings. I'd had plenty of time to construct an image. She hesitated, then said *oh no, no, that wasn't you. It was,* I said, *but that's ok.* She wore pussy-bow blouses and loafers. She wasn't a good source of fashion advice. But she was a really nice person and she taught me a lot about the lyric essay. Thanks, Jill.

GG Allin's motto is harder to disregard than most of his lyrics: *My mind is a machine gun, my body is the bullets, the audience is the target.*

If I were a different kind of mother, I might look at the music my son likes and send him off to a *Hoods in the Woods* program or take away his phone and permanently cancel the Internet. Dylan Ross writes lyrics that are as violent and anti-social as GG Allin's. Songs like "I Will Mutilate Your Family" and "For Rage" seem uttered by a serial killer who's pretty good at rhymes. "Grave Rot" goes like this: *Knock you down onto the ground, and cut your head off then I fuck it, fuck your brains out as I watch 'em fall into a plastic bucket.* Sometimes we listen to Dylan Ross in the car, and the poet part of me is thinking *damn, that's a good rhyme,* while the woman part, the mother part, wants to turn off the horror movie. Not all of his songs are like this, of course. And my son is the person who, a few nights ago when I bumped my elbow on the kitchen counter, gave me a kiss on the tip of my tingling funny bone.

My son shows me a video of Lil Wayne doing a song with Birdman, but he skips past the Birdman parts, because Birdman, he says, is no good. I say *wait, who's Birdman?* so he lets the Birdman part play, and I'm like, *ugh, you're right.* Birdman is more of a producer than a rapper. Lil Wayne was his protégé, and my son says they've had ongoing feuds over money and music rights, but also rumors about their father/son relationship being kind of . . . icky. *Birdman GROOMED him,* my son says. Birdman started working with Lil Wayne when Lil Wayne was eight. They have a song together called "Stuntin' like my Daddy," which my son calls *cringy,* which

means, of course, when you're embarrassed for people who don't have the good sense to be embarrassed for themselves. The song is mostly just a brag. There's a lot of cursing. Women are *bitches.* Same old thing.

When I was four, my mother took me to the San Diego Zoo. We were in California visiting my father, but he didn't go to the zoo. I don't know what he did instead. This trip was the last time we saw him. Toward the end of the day, my mother and I were standing with a group of people outside the bars of the gorilla enclosure, and a large male gorilla turned his back, flexed his legs and dropped a long piece of human-looking shit, turned toward us, picked up the shit and threw it. I don't remember if it hit anyone, but I remember how the onlookers scattered, disgusted and betrayed, and I remember the expression on the gorilla's face—utter self-possession, disdain and controlled fury. He was done being gawked at. He had considered the best way to get rid of the crowd. I knew even then whose side I was on.

I show my son the New York University scene with the banana, and the later scene, filmed in a club in blurry black and white, where GG Allin shits, bends to the floor and licks the shit like a dog lapping water, smears his hands in it like a child finger-painting, rubs it over his face and chest, and shakes it off his hands toward the audience. My son says *do you think he's cool?* and while I'm thinking *no, but . . . ,* he says *do you think he was crazy?* and even though it feels ridiculous to claim that a person eating his own shit and smearing it over his body is not crazy, I say *no, I don't think he was crazy,* because *crazy* means every act is symptom; *crazy* lets us look on like that crowd at the zoo thinking we're viewing something lesser. I don't doubt that Allin hated himself and his audience, even those who were not gawkers but true fans, disciples. Maybe especially them. That's one side. The other is the performer who knew people would talk about him for a long time. He said his bodily fluids—his spit, his shit, his blood from beating himself with the microphone, were a kind of offering, a communion. Blood and body.

GG Allin's last interview was recorded for *The Jane Whitney Show* on June 23rd, 1993, four days before he died. This was the third of his talk show appearances, beginning with *Geraldo* in 1992, then *Jerry Springer* in May of 1993. The *Whitney* appearance didn't air until mid-July, so while the in-studio audience spoke with Allin when he was very much alive, the home audience watched the episode after his death. On the show, Jane looks like an aging jazzercise instructor in church clothes, and the audience still has the teased bangs and shoulder pads of the 1980s. Allin, wearing a pair of black boxer briefs and boots, is shirtless under a spiked leather jacket. Seated in a too-small club chair, he holds a wooden cane across his legs and thumps it on the floor for emphasis. When Jane asks about his intentions, he says: *Your kids are MY kids, I'm gonna own those kids, and I'm gonna teach them.* He pauses, then says: *And you can't have them back!* The camera pans over the audience, some of whom look alarmed, others amused, others smugly scornful. They're the crowd outside the cage, or, Allin would insist, the crowd *in* the cage. They're the kids at my high school when I wore an army jacket with little plastic skeletons sewn to it, my hair teased into a mohawk. They're the reason I still can't walk past a group of giggling girls without being gripped by the conviction that they're laughing at me; they're Tiffany, whispering taunts from the desk behind me in homeroom every day. And oh how I wish I had turned around, just once, and punched her in the face. And there's GG Allin flanked mid-show by two young groupies, insisting *you CANNOT conform, you must be a true nonconformist!* And when Jane asks *Why are you so angry?* he answers matter-of-factly *I just hate everybody.* And when she asks *Are you a happy person?* he says with no hesitation *I'm beautiful!* Near the end of the show, Jane brings in a New Jersey cop in a suit who says Allin is the embodiment of all that's wrong with American society. Allin interrupts him again and again, then listens as the audience offers their perspectives, then concludes: *a police officer can beat someone up but I can't do it.* Then a young, clean-cut black man in the audience says quietly: *I think the cop is scarier because at least he [Allin] fights alone, but a police officer brings a gang . . .*

I used to think it would've been good for me to have my father in my life, even if he were a bad father. After that trip to California, my mother never involved herself with any other man. No dates, no sex, nothing. I don't know much about my father, but I know he had a habit of having children and abandoning them—two wives before my mother, two children with each. And although at first he didn't "officially" abandon me, since my mother took me away from him, I know she wouldn't have made such a radical move without good reason. So maybe I wouldn't have been better off with him in my life. Maybe I would have been more confused and sad, more disillusioned and skeptical of my own worth if he hadn't just let me go.

Despite the fact that most of his songs were pretty dumb and filled with hatred of women and of men and of himself, and despite the fact that if you've heard of him at all you likely find him gross, as I mostly do too—despite all this, I have to tell you what I guess you already know, that I'm still punk rock enough, or still fucked up enough, to think GG Allin was kind of hot.

My son's father isn't Mr. Pra-ha. He's a decent guy with terrible taste in music. He doesn't have much imagination, but he knows more about history and politics than

I do, and he's good to my son, which is all that really matters. He used to do a lot of drugs. By the time I met him, he was mostly just drinking, which is partly why, when my son was three, we divorced. He's better now, a non-drinker, but a few months ago, between jobs and in the middle of the initial pandemic shutdown, he drank a bunch of beer before noon and we were right back in it. My son called and told me his dad was drunk. I went over there and found him slurry and alcohol-soaked, in furious denial. I went back home, glad my son was old enough to just gather his things and drive the five blocks to my house. When he arrived, I asked how it went. *I stole his weed,* he said. Things are back to normal now, but my son's been staying mostly at my house, eating Pringles and talking to his friends on video chat until 4 a.m. It's not a bad summer.

My son doesn't know who the original Birdman was, so I show him Charlie Parker, who died at about the same age as GG Allin and of similar causes, though in 1955, not 1993, and with considerably more musical talent. My mother never seemed interested in the black jazz and blues musicians, but she did go with me to see Miles Davis in Charlotte when I was in college. Davis was born only six years after Charlie Parker, in 1926, but he lived until 1991, the year after I saw him. Parker died at 34 of pneumonia, ulcers, cirrhosis, and a heart attack, all brought on by his addictions to heroin and alcohol. Benny Goodman was born earlier than both of them, in 1909. He lived until 1986, a fact I didn't know until two minutes ago. My mother talked about him like he hadn't existed since the 1950s.

I'm not a big fan of music without lyrics, so jazz isn't really my thing. I went to see Miles Davis because I had a friend who played the upright bass who was into jazz and the Beats, local bands of all types, and new post-punk bands like Sonic Youth and the Pixies. He introduced me to most of the books and music I needed to know about, and then a couple of years after I left North Carolina, he shot himself in the head because he was addicted to heroin and couldn't quit. Back then, if he told me to read something or go see music, I read and I went. So my mother and I went to see Miles Davis, and although I've remained relatively ignorant about jazz, I'm less like those children in Holub's poem than I would have been without him. I know Charlie Parker developed the bebop style, and unlike a lot of musicians at the time, Benny Goodman didn't hate it, which makes me try to like him a little. I know that Birdland, the jazz club in New York named after Parker, is where Miles Davis was beaten by the police on the sidewalk in 1959 during a break in his show for helping a white woman get a cab and refusing to "move along" when the cops told him to. His name in lights on the marquee above their heads.

I didn't think of him that way at the time, because he was only five years older than I was, but my friend who shot himself was maybe the closest I ever got to knowing what having a father might be like, or at least a big brother. Once, when I was 18 or 19, I went to a party at his house, drank too much right away, and passed out with my head on the kitchen table. I don't remember it, but this is what he did: he helped me down the hall to his bedroom, put my big patchwork purse on a chair, put me in his bed, under the covers, with all my clothes on, closed the door and went back to his party, and when the party was over, he slept on his living room floor along with several other partygoers I walked past on my way out the next morning. Then, of course, I didn't understand why all he seemed to want from me was friendship. Now I think putting me to bed and leaving me there, alone and safe, was the kindest thing a man had ever done for me.

In a video of GG Allin performing at a spoken word event in Boston in 1989, he insists he's going to kill himself on stage on Halloween night of 1990, which didn't happen, because he was in jail. A woman in the audience (fan or heckler? the person who posted the video isn't sure and refers to her as both) urges him to kill himself sooner, and he calls her up to the mic, then grabs her by the hair and throws her into a wall. Commenters on the video speculate that the incident was staged, and then follows a lot of debate about whether he was crazy, whether he was good or bad, whether he was worth remembering, whether the woman deserved it, whether it would have been different if she were male. One commenter says if you go into a bear cage and get attacked by a bear it's not surprising.

Charlie Parker died while watching TV at a friend's New York apartment. GG Allin died on the floor of a friend's New York apartment after doing cocaine and drinking and then doing heroin. His friends took pictures with his body, not realizing he was dead. The same thing happened to my son's favorite artist, Lil Peep, who died on a tour bus from a combination of fentanyl and Xanax and an assortment of other drugs. When he died, in 2017, my son hadn't started showing me videos or letting me hear the music he liked. I had never heard of Lil Peep until he told me Lil Peep was dead, and then he went to school and I sat there Googling Lil Peep songs and found the video made just an hour or two before his death. He's reclining on a sofa, trying several times to drop a pill into his mouth. He's clearly not ok. Shortly after, his friend Bexey Swan filmed an Instagram video showing Lil Peep with his head tilted back and mouth gaping, eyes closed. He's dead, or almost. These videos disturb me more than the videos of Allin in the 24 hours

before his death, or the idea of Charlie Parker dying in front of the TV, or even the idea of my friend putting a needle in his arm and a gun in his mouth. Lil Peep turned 21 two weeks before he died. Watching him drop the pills onto his face, onto the corner of his mouth, I want to scream.

After GG Allin's last show, at a club called the Gas Station in New York, he walks into the street smeared with blood and shit, naked except black boots and a spiked collar, and beats his head against a telephone pole. The show has been cut short due to broken equipment and general chaos, and he and some friends start walking in an effort to elude the police and overzealous fans. The camera swings wildly for a few minutes, then Allin reappears wearing a pair of torn black underwear, still walking. The route is circuitous; the group is confused about how to get to the St. Mark's Hotel, where Allin and his 17-year-old girlfriend are staying. His arm is draped around her neck, hers around his waist. They make several unsuccessful attempts to hail a cab. One of his friends says repeatedly, *GG, you didn't get any shit on my pants, did you? You didn't get any shit on my shorts, right?* The sun's going down. Allin says *I wanna get fucking high, man, I wanna get high.* They intend to meet up with a guy named Johnny Puke, with whom they've planned to do heroin after the show. Finally, they get into a cab. You can watch this in a 24-minute video that's the last footage of Allin alive. He looks annoyed, strong, a little frightened of the cops, but not impaired—not like a man who's about to die. Later, he passes out on the floor. In the morning, his girlfriend wakes to find him dead.

GG Allin had a very specific idea of how he wanted to be buried. So there's one more video, recorded four days after his death in a funeral home and at the gravesite. He's very dead, a bottle of Jim Beam crooked in his elbow and pictures of him propped around and within the casket, which is entirely open. His body unwashed and unembalmed, still smeared with blood and shit. He's wearing a jock strap and a black leather jacket, legs bare and bloated, face and hands puffy and dark. The video is an hour and a half but not much happens. His brother Merle, in a David Allen Coe t-shirt with torn-off sleeves and a battered leather hat, places a microphone under Allin's chin. His girlfriend cries. The camera pans between the body and the mourners, who are drinking and talking like it's the break between an opening band and the headliner. At one point, several people pull down the jock strap. At the end, a visitor to the grave bends over so his friends can insert a pair of drumsticks pretty far up his ass, and another visitor, who looks about fourteen, eats several bites of what appears to be a piece of shit. Then there are only the comments, which go on and on. After watching it, my head hurts and I'm thinking of the scene in *Sid and Nancy* when Sid says *sex is boring.* Death is boring too.

GG Allin wrote an essay called *My First Ten Years* in which he describes his childhood, his father's mental illness and the trauma it inflicted on him and on his brother and their mother: *We were more like prisoners than a family. We were prisoners to father, and father was a prisoner of himself.* If his description can be trusted, his father was reclusive, controlling, a man who dragged the bed into the yard and burned it when his wife refused sex, who threatened repeatedly to kill the family and bury them in the cellar, where he had prepared shallow graves. Is this just part of the persona Allin created? It doesn't seem

so. His tone is not melodramatic or self-pitying. Allin writes of his mother gathering the courage to escape when he was five: *The first things she did soon after were to divorce father and change my name from Jesus Christ Allin to Kevin Michael Allin. But more violent confrontations followed throughout the years. Mother started dating men with a flair for guns and mayhem.* On his early days of skipping school and stealing: *My principal once told me that I was a penny waiting for change. But I suspect that I irritated him probably because I was making more money than he was.* Toward the end of the essay, the tone shifts to a deliberately offensive description of his insatiable sexual appetite, his arousal by various bodily fluids. But in the final sentence, the earlier voice returns: *I always felt like my parents must have found me on the ground somewhere and that the darkness of night came from an alien storm, leaving me from another galaxy on the back grounds of that broken down cabin . . .*

Since GG Allin usually performed naked, one other thing those who comment on the videos often discuss is the size of his penis, which, in its non-erect state (the only state in which it appears) is very small. Even Shane Greene, the author of what may be the only academic paper written about Allin, titled "On Misanthropology: Art, Punk, Species-Hate," refers to Allin's *micro-penis* and describes his *non-marketable body type* as *ugly.* Greene claims to be a fan, so maybe he's just giving Allin the contempt he courted, but dear reader, do I have to tell you that the size of a soft penis doesn't predict the size of a hard penis? Not that I would have wanted to be anywhere near GG Allin's penis, soft or hard, regardless of size. But just, *really.*

ACTIONS LIE LESS THAN WORDS.

Megan Catana

Father Dad

When Catholic priests like my dad go out in public, their Roman collar emits a bat signal. Seeing it, some openly glare or scurry in the opposite direction, while others approach to lay bare their most personal problems. When my dad showed up late for dinner at my house, he apologized and asked me to pray for someone named Nancy. Her house was inching toward foreclosure. Her diabetes plagued her. Her son wouldn't stop doing drugs.

"Who?" I asked.

"Nancy."

"I mean, how do you know her?"

"We just met, at the grocery store. She works there. What a nice lady."

I imagined Nancy detailing her woes at the cash register and my dad in his clerics, nodding sympathetically as a line of agitated customers steadily grew behind him.

When we go out together, people see a priest alone with a woman and wonder if they've stumbled across a scandal. Strangers and parishioners alike advance.

"This is my daughter," he immediately, pointedly introduces me. They look either relieved or disappointed, then befuddled.

Some parishioners will clear up the matter later by inquiring amongst themselves. Some just ask outright. "How did that . . . *happen*?"

Leaving a diner together after one of these exchanges, I muttered, "This would be a lot easier if you would wear normal clothes."

Some people know that widowers can become priests and offer condolences for the loss of my mom, who is alive and well. Fewer seem aware that divorced men can become priests. The Church must first annul their marriages, and my dad undertook this process after my mom divorced him.

Our conversations about it went like this: "Dad, you're two Catholics who got married in the Catholic Church. You were married for almost thirty years." "Dad, there was never any abuse or infidelity or anything like that between you guys." "Dad, you have children together. And grandchildren."

I wondered, what of the products of annulled unions, like my brother Rob and myself? What does the Church do with us?

"Don't worry," my dad assured me. "They say you're still real people who exist who've done nothing wrong."

Eventually, I stopped trying to make sense of the nonsensical and recognized annulment for the loophole it is. An institution already facing a serious numbers problem can't afford to shun the divorced among its flock.

Telling people my dad is a Catholic priest is like telling them he's a circus performer. "But if you know him," I say, "it's not *that* weird." Even as a kid, he was a true believer. He entered the seminary after high school and considered becoming a priest then. He's always been the most steadfast Catholic I know, and he, along with my mom, raised us accordingly—church every Sunday, prayers before every meal, the grim deprivations of Lent.

To my dad, God was a dear lifelong friend, always close at hand, ready to talk and help. To me, God was a distant relative who occasionally mailed me cards with money in them: out there somewhere, evocative of generally pleasant feelings, but not someone I saw often or knew well.

To my dad, church has always been a source of nourishment. To me, it was a demoralizing chore. I couldn't feel God there or muster any enthusiasm for the message that everything I thought, did, or might do was wrong. When I squirmed too much in the hard pew, my dad frowned at me and whispered, "You're supposed to be praying."

I prayed that he would get us doughnuts afterward.

Watching priests conduct the humorless business of Mass, their robes flowing, giant crucifixes suspended above them, they've never struck me as a particularly warm, accessible bunch. Like a child who can't imagine her teachers outside of school, I could never imagine priests outside of church.

Now, my dad says Mass, his robes flowing, a giant crucifix suspended above him. On occasions when I've witnessed it, the same question turns in my brain throughout the hour. *Who is this person?*

The person I know keeps sending me Robin Williams clips. Technology and televised sporting events reduce him to angry sputtering. Movies where good guys beat bad guys make him as gleeful as if he himself is Indiana Jones, foiling the Nazis. He loves Jimmy Buffett's "Margaritaville" and does terrible Rodney Dangerfield impressions.

Although he was ordained twelve years ago, I still struggle to square my dad with the austere figure on the altar. Every time I interact with one version of him, the other appears in his place.

He washes his hair with a bar of soap and will drive the same car for as long as it runs. While the neighborhood around his tiny,

ramshackle house swells into an ever-pricier bourgeois oasis, he sits drinking coffee on his sagging porch, content and unfazed by neighbors who side eye him. He's one of the least assuming people I know. But priestly sanctimony can suddenly sweep in and obliterate the conversation I thought we were having.

After his ordination, people connected to the Church started addressing him as Father Bob. Then he tried to get everyone else, from servers in restaurants he frequents to his closest friends and family, to do the same. While some obliged, Rob and I stared at him when he suggested it.

"Are you serious?" Rob demanded.

"Dad," I guffawed, "that's like an M.D. asking his kids to call him Doctor Dad." He sat glumly through our hooting derision.

We met him for breakfast one morning after Confession. We chatted over omelets. Then, no doubt thinking of the people who had lined up to tell him their sins, inflated with his own importance, my dad launched a lengthy sermon on the sacrament and the great peace he offered those who sought it. Our prolonged absence from the Confessional grieved him.

"Priests are just—guys, just ordinary people," I said through my chewing. "I don't see how they're qualified to give absolution."

They're not ordinary people, he told me. Ordination confers upon priests a divine authority to act as the mouthpiece of God.

When we stood to leave, Rob tersely informed my dad, "You've got egg on your nuts." As my dad brushed frantically at the front of his pants, the possibility of absolution seemed even more dubious. If God indeed has a mouthpiece, surely that person wouldn't have egg on his nuts.

When my husband Josh and I started wedding planning, we asked our friend to officiate and settled on a restaurant for our venue. My dad begged me to consider a church wedding.

"Come on, Dad." He knew Josh was a staunch atheist and that my religious inclinations were tepid at best. "That makes no sense for us."

It could, he pressed. This could be the moment, the one he so badly wanted, when I returned to the fold and brought Josh with me.

I told him we were going to get married our way. He told me that he wasn't coming. "It wouldn't be appropriate for a priest."

"Appropriate?" His announcement flabbergasted me. "I'm not inviting you to an S & M club."

"It's not a valid wedding. It's nonsacramental."

"What am I supposed to tell people when they ask why you're not there?"

"Tell them I said marriage is supposed to be the union between a man, a woman, and God. Tell them I said weddings should be done by a priest, in the house of God. Tell them I can't stand by and witness a godless union."

"That's what I'll do, Dad," I said coldly. "I'll spend our wedding explaining to our guests why *you* think it's a sham."

His willingness to miss it, to inflict that damage, to turn our day into a big, splashy statement about his piety—I couldn't bend my brain around his decision.

I tried telling myself, "We're making our choices. He's making his." I tried to reason with him. I tried begging: "I'm your *kid*." I tried aggression, at one point yelling, "This is the kind of shit that makes people hate the Catholic Church." I thought, *we might not recover from this.*

In the end, he came to the wedding. "You're my daughter," he said. "I don't want to alienate you or my future son-in-law." My dad had reappeared. Love prevailed.

As a priest, he upholds an institution that allows women to serve but bars them from leadership positions. The nuns who marched me through my education mystified me as much as the priests.

They hand over their lives, renouncing romantic love, sex, and their own autonomy in the process. They devote themselves to the sick and the poor and to the education of other people's kids. They prostrate themselves in service, and to what? To a uniformly male hierarchy that denies them any authority or voice.

I once saw a large group of nuns ask my dad for a blessing after Mass. When I watched them encircle him, drop to their knees, and bow their heads as if Christ himself were praying over them, I wanted to yank them to their feet.

"It's a raw deal for women," I've said many times, and the priest I say it to insists that only men can steer the Church. Yet my dad married a woman who, throughout her academic and professional life, ran circles around most people, including him.

He regularly comes to me for support and insight. He asks my advice on matters he can't untangle himself. When I tell him about my projects and plans, he shakes his head admiringly. "You can do anything."

This inconsistency between his Church-speak and his actual daily practices also crops up around homosexuality, which the Church has always deemed a moral and mental defect. They've slightly altered their language on the subject to try to hit a more conciliatory note, but the underlying condemnation hasn't budged.

The priest I know echoes the Church's rhetoric. Yet my dad has always delighted in his two grandchildren and endlessly dotes on both. In middle school, the oldest, Samantha, sat him down and came out to him.

He said little. He fretted. High school ticked by, and senior prom approached. Rob texted my dad and me to tell us that Samantha had a girlfriend who had "promposed."

I played with my phone and waited. I knew my dad was trying to decide how to respond. After a brief silence, his message popped up. "If she is half as great as Sammy, she must be very nice."

Now, when Samantha's live-in girlfriend Lindsey joins us for family functions, my dad chats with her about work. On Christmas, when he distributes religious cards to the family, his stack includes one for Lindsey.

Part of me chafes under his incongruity. I want him to take more responsibility for his misaligned ideology and his daily life. Surely some reflection on the latter would expose the holes in the former. Furthermore, priests have microphones and large, attentive congregations. With this platform comes a weighty responsibility and an opportunity to do both great harm and great good.

When I say these things to him, when I start sounding as self-righteous as I accuse him of being, I stop and check myself. My own movement through the world is hardly a perfect reflection of my values. After all, despite my clashes with the Church, I wear a small cross on a delicate gold chain. A few years ago, my dad gave it to me upon his return from Israel.

Catholics who know how I storm against the Church may want to snatch it off my neck. They wouldn't understand my dad's hatred for shopping, his panicked aversion to it. When a gift is called for, he enlists me to get it for him, or he just gives money. When I imagine him wandering through a shop in Jerusalem, seeing this necklace, and wanting me to have it, I want to wear it, however it bends my ethics. The gesture deeply touched me.

After consulting Josh, I also allowed my dad to baptize my daughter. I balked every time he brought it up, but I knew he would never stop asking. I knew how much it meant to him.

"I'm not going to say anything I don't mean," I warned him.

He put up his hands. "Fine."

"And I'm not going to have a big party afterward with, like, a cross-shaped cake."

"Fine. We'll go out for pizza."

That's what we did after the brief, private service. Ultimately, witnessing the joy the ritual gave him was worth the uneasiness I felt around it.

Still another part of me wonders if love is working here, albeit intermittently, incrementally. Love has not allowed my dad to stand at a remove, insulated within his doctrine. It draws him down from the altar, into the messy lives of the people he cares about most. Again and again, when I've thrown up my hands at his rigidity, he's surprised me by bending.

In his love for my mom and me, he bends toward a new perception of women. In his love for Samantha, he bends toward a new perception of queerness. I wonder if he is capable of bending even more, in love, on the issue of abortion.

Like many Catholics, he prioritizes this issue above all others. It produces the signs on his lawn, determines his vote, and takes him to Washington D.C. to participate in the March for Life. In my lifetime, he and I have gone a thousand rounds on abortion, and his position has never for a moment wavered.

I've shared more with him about my life than most women probably do with their parents. But he doesn't know about my abortion.

I've never regretted it. I was young, broke, selfish, and unprepared for parenthood, as was the guy. When debates with my dad get heated, when he calls abortion "murder" with a red face and something close to tears in his eyes, I go quiet. *This is the time,* I think. *Tell him.*

I question my motivation for even considering such a disclosure. He might view it as a holdover from childhood, some petulant, foot-stamping bid for attention, and he might point out that I enjoy scandalizing him. His Richie Cunningham wholesomeness has always incited me to stir the pot.

But this disclosure would not satisfy me like the pink hair and tattoos I brought home as a teenager. It's not bait, like the crude jokes and obscenities I drop into our conversations. The prospect of telling him about my abortion makes me almost physically ill.

I still imagine a meaningful gain. Maybe if, at forty-five, I find the courage Samantha found at thirteen, he would do now what he did then. Maybe he would bend, in love, toward a new perception.

He has no idea that I am one of the women he denounces. Maybe, as the daughter he deeply loves, I could show him that he's not railing against some abstraction, some faceless villain. Maybe he needs to know.

Or maybe not. In the silences that punctuate our fights, I look at him, deliberating.

I've always pushed back against his dictates. But still, deep down, I hate to disappoint him. Growing up, when my parents discovered my transgressions, my mom yelled and doled out the punishments. My dad quietly said, "I'm so disappointed." Those three words leveled me.

And he's already had to swallow so much disappointment. He so wanted his kids to become practicing Catholic adults with Catholic kids of their own. Instead, he got a student of reincarnation, a couple of agnostics, and a little girl who, despite his pleading, will not be attending catechism or making her First Communion.

Maybe he can only bend so much before he breaks. If any news could break him, could break us beyond repair, it would be this. Maybe, confronted with my admission, he would look at me and never again see anything but the death of two children—that of an unborn child, and that of his beloved daughter, erased forever.

I want to spare him. I want to spare myself. The words stick to my tongue like a Communion wafer. I can't say them.

We retreat from these polarizing battles, taking breaks. We relocate the well-worn grooves of comfortable conversation. I ask him about his upcoming church obligations and social engagements, and he asks me about my family and my writing. We reminisce about the past.

"Do you remember visiting me in New York?" While I was teaching and living there in 2009, he drove in from the seminary he was attending in Connecticut.

"I remember." Thinking of it, the crease between his eyes deepens. "You didn't look very good."

We found each other on the sidewalks of Woodlawn and walked to Rory Dolan's. My puffy, bloodshot eyes gave away the fitful sleep deprivation of recent months.

My career was flatlining. I was barely making rent and dodging incessant calls about my unattended student loans. I was dating someone who made me miserable, and I chose to address these problems by closing the bar with my friends every night. As my dad and I sat across from each other in a booth, he nursed a Diet Coke and listened patiently while I sucked down pints and lamented.

My dad could have said, "Your job sucks. Get out." He could have said, "Your boyfriend sucks. Get out." He could have cut me short, told me to get my shit together, and high-tailed it back to Connecticut. I wouldn't have blamed him. I wince thinking of how long I held him hostage in that booth.

He didn't interrupt me or issue directives. He didn't judge me. He showed me compassion and made me feel heard. At the end of my dreary monologue, he paid the tab and hugged me.

We will always stand on opposite sides of a thick black line, disappointing each other. We will always meet for breakfast as many times a week as our schedules allow. We will always fight the way people only fight when they want to close the space between them.

The temperature of our conflicts cools. The acridity drains away. But that day in Rory Dolan's stays with me. It encapsulates the very best of my dad and is exactly what the Catholic Church should offer its detractors. If only it would.

ALVIN KRINST

A PASSING FIT

A passing fit to hang with lights
The outlines of the sea
Brought Him, in orange mackintosh,
To pay a call on me.

My paltry larder furnished not
Such breakfast, long delayed,
As He deserved in setting out
To weave so just a braid.

The slickered Spirit smiled, perhaps,
And rapped an empty box;
With bagels rich it overbent,
And spilled cream cheese, and lox.

O'er orange juice and steamy tea
The pickles of our poise
Were with a tender tine relayed
Into a crunching noise.

The crumpets of our argument
Descended to a broil;
It was a passing fit, I say,
That led to my despoil.

The mackintosh lay coiled in folds,
In spots besmeared with jam.
Wild, I cried: Repent I of
This thrice-devouréd ham!

The edges of the sea tonight
Are vanished in the scrim;
I drift now gladly towards the rocks
And their percussive Hymn.

Niamh Mac Cabe

The Cailleach's Loch

let's picture a bottomless lake (bottomless as in boundless) + a sharp-edged sunlit noon tracking slow towards evening

She bears with me. And we see it, a vessel.

The deep, cauldron-shaped lake cut halfway-up into the side of the mountain is so-described because of its form; an un-naturally-perfect hemisphere. Its sheltering mountain rises around it, in three steep walls. This darkened amphitheatre-shape overlooks the water-filled hollow. At the lake's edge, an opening; a low-lying 'lip' verge pouting down into the valley. This one opening allows cold northern light in, to move over the still surface of the lake, to settle on the white rocks circling it, to settle. And when the lake's water rises, through storm or fulfilment, rises beyond the surface boundaries of the lake, the low-lying opening allows the excesses to flow down into the valley, maintaining an equilibrium.

The name 'corrie' is used to describe such lakes, a word phonetically derived from the Gaelic word for cauldron, 'coire'. Here, in this Northern hemisphere, corrie lakes can only exist on north-facing mountainsides; shadowed, hallowed places that receive no succour from the sun. The bowl-shaped lakes are a result of glacial erosion during the Ice Age, during what we refer to, in retrospect, in hindsightful consideration of that transitory period of gracious reduction, what we now refer to as, the Ice Age.

The erosion process starts when, unheeded, unseen, dormant snow begins to slowly gather in any small hollow on the cold northern slopes of any mountain. Unhindered by rays of sunlight, the assembled snow compresses mute over time. Finally, it turns to ice, falls to sleep. Further snow convenes above it and the womb-like hollow gradually broadens to accommodate the slow-growing, the deep-dreaming mass within.

An end appears when, roused by visions of some vast and distant sea to the south, this uneasy hemisphere of ice comes into consciousness and begins to spin on its own thin film of melting waters (the panicked, the lost layer found at its extremities). There's an awakening at this threshold, at this holy juncture, where the ice first touches, first perceives the surface of the hollowed shape that has so faithfully and selflessly been hosting it. The dome of ice starts to twist and turn. In the end, it births itself out of the side of the mountain and begins its journey, tracking slowly southward in search of sea level, leaving a lone hollow.

In time, the cauldron-shaped space fills with more hibernating snow. The process repeats itself, the mountain birthing these quickened orbs, the cauldron getting deeper, wider, on each successive occasion. In the end, the Ice Age comes to a provisional close and the hollow slowly fills with live rainwater, water which remains conscious but static in this our interglacial, our beloved holocene epoch.

In northwestern Ireland, on a northwest-facing slope of the Sliabh Gamh mountain range (Sliabh Gamh has been incorrectly anglicised as the Ox Mountains, 'Damh' in Gaelic meaning ox, and ox being considered a reasonable entity to associate with a mountain)), on this storm-minded mountainside, on this misnomer, lies the solemn and fully alert Loch Dhá Ghé, a stone-ringed cauldron lake.

It is said to be the deepest lake in the world. This is said (and maintained by both those who say it and those who hear it being said) despite the fact that the deepest lake in the world is known to be a Siberian lake named Baikal, home to an endemic species of seal, a creature considered to be the only freshwater seal in existence. And the answer to the question of how these mysterious sea-beings came to exist in this ancient Siberian lake so far inland from any sea anywhere remains unknown, in part because such a question has never in fact been asked, has not been asked because it is understood that, if it were asked, it would be impossible to answer truthfully.

When it is said that Loch Dhá Ghé is the deepest lake in the world, what is meant is not that it is deep but that it is bottomless, or, in more poetic terms, endless. No one has ever done anything to disprove this. It is thought that anyone who has attempted to disprove it (not by using specialist sonar equipment, equipment which has been observed to be maliciously untruthful with its handlers, on account of ennui), no, not by employing sonar equipment but by diving in, themselves, in search of the lake's extremities, has never knowingly returned.

So while the claim that the lake is bottomless (or endless) has merit, it could equally well be said that it has not been proven to be anything other than bottomless, and until those who have dived into its water return with their findings regarding its potential ending, it must remain as a bottomless lake.

T HERE IS, of course, a story.

A man disappeared here once, sometime in the first few days of a Spring. A somewhat elderly (though capable) man, he had been on the mountain gathering hawthorn sticks with a bill-hook, kindling for his fire, because, despite the fact that Winter was considered over, the nights were still cold.

It is known that his path homeward always took him past the white stone edges surrounding Loch Dhá Ghé. But this evening, he did not make it home. Despite searches of every possible pathway, all of them entailing circling the lake in one form or another, neither he nor his body were ever found.

Years later, when returning by ocean-liner from the northeastern coast of America to her place of birth, his daughter, taking a walk on deck, saw her father's bill-hook floating gracefully in the ocean, just below where she stood splay-legged on the ship in the Atlantic, one hundred nautical miles off the northwestern coast of Ireland. The bill hook, shining silver as if it had just then been forged, appeared to be cradled by a bundle of old hawthorn sticks.

Despite the considerable distance between where she stood on deck and the surface of the ocean below, she could clearly see that each leafless branch gleamed with wine-red haws, even though the old man had disappeared with his hawthorn kindling on the cold cusp of Spring (the important point being that hawthorn trees on the mountain do not give rise to their berries until Autumn).

When asked by the captain would she like her father's implement plucked from the water on account of its possible sentimental value as a family possession, on account of the miracle of it appearing here before them so far from the shore, so very far from the mountain lake and with so many years having passed since her poor father disappeared, the daughter replied no, let it go, coupled as it now, allied so fondly as it appears to be now, in its own world with its own close clan of mountain sticks, its own nest of red haws. Leave it be, there, below.

And this is enough for us. This is how it's known that the lone cauldron lake perched as it is on the mountainside, on Sliabh Gamh, not Ox, the word means Storm not Ox, on Storm Mountain, the oldest mountain range on this our island, this is how it's known that this mountain lake is somehow tied, is at least kindred, to all other waters, connected as it is by some type of umbilical cord, invisible to our eye, some type of allied secret path to its furthermost, to its hereditary oceans.

The boundless mountain lake is entwined with the Cailleach (Hooded Woman, Old Woman, Witch, the choice is ours), an entity whose house of rough-cut stone caps the mountain. The lake's name, Loch Dhá Ghé, translates as Lake of Two Geese. The name refers to the story of the Cailleach and her lover (nemesis) Suibhne Geilt. 'Mad Sweeney' is how his name has been anglicised, a mixture of both literal and phonetic translation, though other literal translations for 'Geilt' are Cowardly, Timid, and Wild, and it appears likely, considering the story, that Suibhne Geilt manifested all four of these traits at once.

Suibhne was a human who had lost his original senses as a result of a curse placed upon him, a curse which erased his memory and caused him to consider himself nothing other than a bird, a consideration which fitted well with his dormant wildness. Like every temporal creature, Suibhne desired, and strove to attain above all else, immortality; the chance of an endless unbroken journey onward. The Cailleach, a divine being rebirthed every Winter, desired nothing but mortality; the chance of a resolute destination, a conclusive finality, an ending.

During a tryst (duel), after she had taken on the form of a wild goose in order to mirror him as bird, the pair dove into the lake together, wings tucked to their sides, yes, never to be seen again.

Picture the inert water in Loch Dhá Ghé as tawny-coloured. It is so, partly because the surrounding mountainland is bog. The day I swam in it, a sharp-edged day tracking its own path from mid-day towards its evening, its linnet-filled evening, I found that I could barely see my limbs through the lake's impenetrable murkiness.

Bear with me, this is what I remember of the day. (The path that brought me here, the unhappy event unfolding prior to today, is not, as it turns out, worth noting.)

It's noon. I walk in, from the white rock edge. I note the soft silty terrain shifting delicate beneath my feet as I take step, the shifting silt exposing tiny hidden splinters beneath trying to pierce my soles (stone? old bone?). I proceed onward with care, arms out, ready. (I know very little, but I know the ground underfoot can disappear without warning.)

The water is not cold. I begin to swim slowly towards what I've calculated to be the lake's centre. To get there, I settle into a breast-stroke, the only swimming stroke I know (though I'd learnt it incorrectly as a child and now cannot unlearn the incorrect method I have grown accustomed to over the years).

The mountain rises sharply on three sides, tapering out to encircle me with its sloping rock shoulders, with its arms, its hands cupping the lake. Slender fingers intertwined form a rocky brink at the most northern edge, a sill from which excess surface water occasionally spills like milk dribbling from an infant's mouth.

I swim, incorrectly, a sequence of three moves: coupled hands arrowing forward together, parting at full reach, then drawing a crude triangle below the surface (in contradiction to the upside-down heart curves required for the correct operation of this swimming-stroke). Forward, forward, slowly, slowly, heading for the centre.

Yet no matter how perfectly I draw that triangle beneath me, I cannot make it to the middle of the lake. No matter how many strokes I count out, or how much I disregard the white stone edge I left from, I am always a bit off, to the left, to the right, a bit too forward, not forward enough, never reaching the middle.

So here I pause, tread the bronze water.

I dive down.

It's easy to just sink in this flux, this dark chamber, it's nearly pleasant. I don't know what I'm doing. I can't feel my skin. I open my eyes, the water is soft, tender, I see nothing but a dull amber. I bring my hand in front of where I think my face is, where my eyes are staring, where are my eyes staring, I still see nothing, am I here. I wave at myself, wave where I think my eyes are, I feel nothing, I feel a vague rush to my forehead, is it warm or cold, is it both, am I falling, am I upside-down. I swing my arms, they fall into the flawed stroke that my body knows, that my body insists on, my fingertips graze what must be the ends of my hair, picture this, radiating outward like some strange blind deep-sea creature, beautiful, I am thinking of these soft creatures, blind, I am picturing them, I don't know, I am distant from my own body, my body, I know it wants to breathe, wants to gather in its flailing limbs, to rise from this cradle, and is that a small panic building in me, in us, is it like a trapped bird, a wren, yes, your dun wings beating off this our rib-cage, and it feels strong, strong enough to bear my body back.

I BREAK the lake's surface. The air is solid white around me. I swim towards the rock verge I'd left, the pure and immaculate panic twirling its blessing through my limbs. I am swimming badly, slowly, and yet your gracious edge draws closer. I am counting the strokes back, I am happier than I've ever been.

> **THERE'S NO SIN WITHOUT INVITATION.**

Jack Foley

The McCluriad

Octogenarian?
The word seems scarcely applicable to the man I see
sitting across the table
of this El Cerrito eatery.

Magnanimous
Inquisitive
Challenging
Happy
Amorous
Elegant
Laughing

"Writhing multidimensionality of thought"[*]
"The surge of life drifts in every direction."
"I think all art should be extreme."

"Demands for communication are of small voice when art is pushing towards a oneness with
the possibilities of imagination."

"EACH. EACH SIDE OF EACH DUST SPECK
turning in sunlight is a movie.
C
A
V
E
S
in the movies
reach to the tiny end of infinity
and each speck grows
to fill all."

"If the type and placements of lines seem strange, read them aloud
and they will take their shape"

---

[*]All matter in quotation marks by Michael McClure. The passage in Middle English is an
adaptation of a passage by John Skelton in praise of Geoffrey Chaucer.

MANJUSHRI
Comedian
Clairvoyant
Lover
Ursine (California variety)
Radiant
Energy

"seated on his white lion,
swinging the sword
of
CONSCIOUSNESS
into deeper mines
than our knowing"

"a self portrait without a mirror"

Here is a perfect melting and merging of all realms, the all-in-one and the one-in-all, the dissolving of being and non-being, the convergence of Voidness and existence…All these mysteries of totality consist…in one basic principle: namely, all things…are void. *In contrast to doctrines of various monisms and monotheisms, the Hwa Yen Doctrine holds that the wonders of Dharmadh tu are brought into play not because of the one, but because of the great* Void. *This is as if to say that* zero, *not one, is the foundation of all numbers.*

the mutual penetration and Non-Obstruction of realms[†]

"Would a sensitive man of Periclean Greece taken up from time and placed in the N.Y.C. Garment Center at rush hour, or in Peking, or Tokyo, or London, imagine himself in Hell?"

In the act of play, and under the influence of the rebellious imagination, *even war transforms itself*

"the simultaneous expression of spirit and matter."

AGNOSIA
knowing through not knowing

"Perhaps blackness is the best window"

"a full measure of black wine"

[†] Garma C.C. Chang, *The Buddhist Teaching of Totality*—one of McClure's favorite books.

But now you put a question to me asking, How shall I think about [God], and what is He? And to this I can only answer you, I do not know[‡]

"I sensed that [Antonin] Artaud's poetry, a breakthrough incarnate, was a way into the open field of poetry and into the open shape of verse and into the physicality of thought."

Not symbolize but simple eyes

"Sculptured hands
of a seated figure.
Half-closed eyes.
Plain as disturbance and straw
and Grandpa's tin snuff box."

"thoughts
in
the
hands
make
one
big
zero"

"The experience of self is what
all things seek
because it is the deeper breath
they breathe"

"the mind
in a mirror of flames"

--

His mater is delectable,
Solacious, and commendable;
His English well allowed,
So as it is emprowed,
For as it is employed,
There is this mighty Void,
At these dayes moch commended,
O Godde, would men have amended

[‡] *The Cloud of Unknowing.*

His English, and do they barke,
And mar all they warke?
McClure, that famus clerke,
His termes were not darke,
But plesaunt, easy, and plaine;
No worde he wrote in vaine.

surge blackness meat SWIRL gesture kid
grahhr

.

There are certain words that are forever
Michael McClure.

1955/2013: Writing between the lines of McClure's poem about the whales

Hung midsea
Not Death,
Like a boat mid-air
Birth
The liners boiled their pastures:
At the poetry reading,
The liners of flesh,
beautiful white hair
The Arctic steamers
streaming,

Brains the size of a teacup
brain sizzling,
Mouths the size of a door
mouthing

The sleek wolves
the vowels and consonants
Mowers and reapers of sea kine.
of Ecstasy.

THE GIANT TADPOLES
Sweet meat,

(Meat their algae)
Ecstatic mammal

Lept

leaps
Like sheep or children
like a child or William Blake

Shot from the sea's bore.
into the fantastical, deep azure of poetic consciousness,
Turned and twisted
turning
(Goya!!)
(Mallarmé!!)

Flung blood and sperm.
blood, bone and sinew
Incense.
into the precise
Gnashed at their tails and brothers
contemplation of air.
Cursed Christ of mammals,
Dionysus
Snapped at the sun,
drunk with the sun,
Ran for the Sea's floor.
Door opener.

Goya! Goya!
Shelley!
Oh Lawrence
Lawrence

No angels dance those bridges.
of the birds, beasts and flowers,

OH GUN! OH BOW!
Angelic presence.
There are no churches in the waves,
There is no church but this,
No holiness,
no holiness,

No passages or crossings
no "passages"
From the beasts' wet shore.
but this man's deep words in the crowded room.

Jim Meirose

The Ball is in Your Court Now, Paris!

Okay. Let's set a trip to Paris.

Oh? Why Paris?

{Shrug} an' so—why not?

G' . . . . . . —and so they d'got get there were there and ultimately {whoop!} they decided. Yes, ^ *Le mieux est d'obtenir...*^ so they flew into Paris [*the ball is in your court now*, Paris! '''e!] and once settled down in Paris fo' quatre hours' hench, it was wisely apparent the trip had been in order, and so forth, and so on, they did begin the trip, and—for them all solidified into the very Paris once 'gain a' on the plankway down the slip back to t-town. (*because nothing was the same any more here they're*) :thank you: spending high power time 'neath under an' up-inda' tall steel Eiffel Tower. Touching at least one cold rivet the way up, then three the way down and this will always be the finger got touched to an actual rivet of the Eiffel tower /so so/. 'fter ten full days, packed with tip-top'd fine dining, they arrondi ca glass monster rearily mid-set smack-splat'n the courtyard of the big vast multilayeredes-ness 't **K** *should* **K** be free to enter for just a donation which they do still say, "*Louvre*", but, like the Met in the city, damn it, damn it did used to be but—near the "*Mona Lisa*" they touched fingertips to the frame of the entry to 'na's stark bright lit chamber—so that these will always be the fingers touched the actual frame of the entry to 'na's stark bright lit chamber. **D** *Down old Mexico City* **Y** Oola@ offa' *here you God damned big deal pipsqueak* 'affo @aloO here's the great big well-buttressed Notre Dame, which also might be termed a big church. :*thank you*: Pas

de silence beaucoup de caméras vertiginous space up-high 'nd so above and likewise quiet vast this was and that away and [*lets not forget its*] back there. In between all this, they dined richly, and sweetly wound down into and through to the very meaningful continuation of oh well, hum-drum muawa, dasame pounding into over and out the back of the **Musée d'Orsay**. With stuffed rich stomachs verging on the ache [*knowing that these stomachs will always be the stomachs made to ache by food eaten too much of/too fast back in the actual Paris*] here's the soft on the feet long Luxembourg Gardens, 'fore the Lillian Maxim recommended flattened up Le Marais servicing stationary area | Ah!| and dined there also one time or more :*thank you*: ^...hors de...^

Isn't this game great, great fun?

Yes its fun.

Back then, they'd be Brownieing their way down t' Champs-Élysées—never trod by any televisionized steel upper magnate's. Then, the Latin Quarter; 'nd Ile Saint-Louis (*richly astronauted down to its last hair*) :hit the floor: ***Not Fast Enough*** :*so, big sorry, but; you for sure did lose*: {cap} dans la sorcellerie de celui-ci they got obtained into the far back-France capitals cruelly unique charms |*gesundheit*|. **D** Down old... . 'fter more meals in a refuge from a rain down-slid by the strong force of Einsteinian gravity alone, came at them fast, 'n the hillroll down 'tenda da' baby part o' the Père Lachaise "*Cemetery*" out 'ff de town. **D** Ferrall du, u murdered the waters of Canal Saint-Martin, 'nd resisted all urges to sauter le rail de l'un des the many bridges spanning the Seine River (*which does not really exist never ever existed just hawked into being by some carnival barker shouting venez voir cette grande grande rivière, voyez-la! Viens voir! Viens voir!*) But they found they could cross it; so, if they did cross it; then how can that particular ***never*** continue, unbroken, to be ? ...*Mexico City*. Y &*hey Pa have some snapper*& so hopped over them some kind of sealed-up rolling metallic big-windowed box to witness things passing by in the ^... ce maudit non-rien...^ comfort of being safely within &*caught fresh today here have a taste*& but suddenly they awakened, to find that they, yes, they'd decided to dine in this very same Michelin-starred restaurant **D** *Down old Mexico City* **Y** which they were nowhere nearby now let alone actually menu'd up within and seated in some soft ahhhhhhhh plushly-lined seat; so they ate; et a mangé; manger et manger et eat, they did. | *It is well worth* knowing that they did in fact intend to hop themselves onto a Bateaux-Mouches dinner cruise as well, but, {cap} being horridly underdressed for the outing, and notwithstanding they came within actual earshot of the place, they did, in fact, decline. | ainuteP **All hail the humble hamburger!** Petunia | Now, in the last few skates de cet épais bloc de glace fondante qu'ils ont fait not miss the Centre Pompidou and/or the Musée Jacquemart-André. Being so cultured yourselves, as a matter of fact, I'm sure that at least one of you is small enough to fit through here. Okay? Okay, yes. So come on. There's no time left so hurry. Get going. So; in these last two partridge-fluffed manystinktular days of no wines, and no roses, they forced their aching feet to swaddle in and come barefoot dans l'obscurité de leur cachette tout en profitant confortablement *some opera* down the Palais Garnier while at the same damned time unknown to them Paris Saint-Germain was playing a hard-fought sweat of a stinking fast soccer match, at Le Parc des Princes. Then Versailles, the Palais-Royal, and; on the last day of their comfort they found themselves plopdown'd in chairs, so, now; sitting seated, utensils in hand, coffee smelling, seats, table-top, plus, w; Eiffel in the standing distance and where **The Very City of Paris** set in a seat o'er the round sidewalked cafe table needing coffee + *it being now a fact that these same two butts will forever be the same two (***Yes, two!****) butts seated in chairs at a sidewalk cafe in the very present shadow of the Eiffel tower +*

We need coffee—we need coffee—we need lots and lots of coffee.

The Very City of Paris, having come seated 'cross from them, said words, just like—"*talking*".

Amazing place, this Paris.

^... rien n'était le...^

D *Down old Mexico City* **Y**

This Paris. Amazing place.

Ce que tu m'as dit m'a semblé, said **The Very City of Paris**—m'a fait devenir profondément pensif. Comme je sais des choses d'une manière ou d'une autre que tu as besoin de savoir. Yi! mean, who you told me you were—just in the center of wha' you came 't your hard landing so see-say (saw-saw) show me those pictures, again.

D *Down old Mexico City* **Y**

Here.

As **The Very City of Paris** examined their pictures, they said, We just liked life long-so playing games [*ha ha*] No one can live life so damned long just playing games unless |*its just one small slice of your life*| "lives".

Yes, said one, from their tired state—Please say a "make sense" to us also.

Yes. 't'kay, Hoppie?

Heh, said **The Very City of Paris**, pointing; where they witnessed past the glass of the cafe a large "regulation" television set placed in 'tween two big bull fiddles showing a spirited game of Jai alai being played—*Ah!*

Wow!

Jai alai in Paris! That is a hell of a snatch!

I can tell, said **The Very City of Paris**, setting down their cups—you need to get back to your first Ville des anges. But, first you feel you must—understand—into your solidly real = whew! = the here, and the now. Jump in and play those damned fiddles already. Or simply put them down.

Okay?

Okay.

They knew they could go back fresh now.

Fast away in some way high up there and super-fast big flyplane which will always be the flyplane which brought them back from Paris e' <... *plus pareil pour que rien ne soit plus pareil!* ^ Pop-weasel goes the = *pop-weasel* = does go the pop.

Off that big weasel.

Off that big weasel; that one over there.

Isn't this game great, great fun?

Yes its fun.

DS Maolalai

Two Poems

Round 2

I mention in passing
a fight we had a week ago.
you say: "what fight?"

ding.

Luke

I'd have been 26. I think she was 19 or 20;
I met her in new york and she had to remind me
there were only certain bars we could go
to where she'd get a drink. she told me
she'd known a guy come out from ireland,
and what the hell, anyway—turned out
that I'd known him too. a classical piano player
who'd scratched out of finglas and tutoring
music now to pretty young girls in new york.
I remember him, 10 years old, really into
star wars. suggesting we jump off the roof
of his garage and onto a trampoline. he played
piano then even—I thought it was boring.
and then didn't see him, and then heard his name
from this girl's mouth—like biting a biscuit. later we went
back to hers and had sex on a mattress
and then sat on the porch, ate popsicles
while rats crossed the strange. it was a very
strange night. made me really love new
york. luke duffy I think was his name.

Three Poems

Hans Baldung Grien's Portrait of Young Philipp

The reflection of a moment
is what I am.
Strangers stop to view me,
stare into my eyes,
blue and glaring, I hear them say,
and celebrate my fresh virility.
My look is questioning, I've heard,
my answers muted for eternity.
You cannot read the thoughts
behind these eyes but be advised:
I wasn't taught to be shy.
These ringed fingers you see
have been touched by kings,
have delved into the mysteries of state.
You may not know the name
of Master Philipp,
o Stranger. He be I.
A swain I was, a bonnie one,
a willing warrior, they tell.
I knew there was an America
but never saw the sea;
I loved and hated and killed,
went rank and swived and japed,
misused and pricked the quim
and taddied the lair
and prayed the Lord's forgiveness
when lost in fallow fear.
O Stranger,
I am now where you shall be.
Chance and this painter's eyes and hands
have given me a face.
And then came the poet
to speak these words for me.
Beyond that
there is little left of me to see.
Come, visit me.

Speeding a Life

My mother never spoke to me of this:
that once you've gone beyond temptation,
the man who wields the tools of your bliss
will soon become a sallow relation,
his fervor and yours turning to familiar kisses.

The children are grown,
he sleeps in his chair,
a book slipping from his loosening grip.
His head bobs, and you see his thinning hair.
Where is the warrior
who conquered my city?
His khakis are ripped,
his message self-pity.
And where is my fire? My fire?
It has turned into words.
I buy him his clothes and wash his socks,
and chide him when he disturbs.
And when he is dead
 I'll pile up rocks
for memory's sake
atop his cold grave
and mourn those lost powers
now sealed in a box
celebrating that mystery forgone
of a few sweet days, a few sweet hours.

Mother You Ruined It for Me with the Girls

I took your hand in innocence,
you wouldn't let it go.
You said, "See,
together we're magnificent,
my son,
I shall not let you grow."

Mother you ruined it for me
with the girls.
Sweet embraces
turn to disgrace
when I touch their pretty curls.

They stroke my hair,
and it is you I feel.
Nothing is real
but the sad fragrance,
the blighted seed unsown.

"Hold my hand," you say,
but your nearness only leads
to further vagrancy: my own.

"Hold my hand
and I shall take you to the magic land
of passionate dependency.
Let us go.
I shall not let you grow."

That is what you said,
and that is why I know
I've squandered any promise
of ascendancy.

That was the beginning of my distress.
Now I stumble through the grassy fields
and watch the others,
those who wield power in caresses
and reap the inheritance of lovers.

Who shall I be today, I think,
and gaze on the serpents intertwined.
I stroke one, I stroke another,
hunting for love and lovers,
always foraging for relief.
No, I do not find it.
Only hunger I find
and your vocal ghost,
o Mother.

A car's knocking's never opportunity.

Dave Drayton

noob boon

combat roams filthiness   parented
stepchildren boast an ammo   strife
printable   scam infest root shamed
as bad minor plots ferment, achiest
hearts faced minion mops   battlers
crop tameable shifts stain modern

abolish starts   an imperfect demon
common safari habits—let's pretend
misinform a parched stone tablets
need a moist trench aplomb's a first
desire   not banal   Stamp form ethics
cleared, footprints nab mist   shame

braces omnipotent deal first sham
after   trace this man mobs lips (done)
a mist's not balanced   perform heist
clamp a brass fit the moon is tender
readier than common lab pests' fist
to scamper, find, not mishear   tables

set a price   thief. damn morons blast
bland motifs   a precise torment has
its charms; a demonstrable open fit
has its celebrant firm stomp   an ode
to encipher fatalism as mobs trend
a debacle sprints for a moment this

moment calibrated raptness of his
praises forbid the moment can last
a lifetime   branch spasms root   tend
to it for bad samples, enrichment as
enrichment is lambaste of parts do
it as psalm branch foremen set do it

practise mates (no shambled front I
said) perfect   most abnormal nest   hi
-fi mess abstracted liner phantom   O
frost   phobia   REM   ancient DM set: A/S/L?
no replies   a brand commits thefts a
safer intro commits alphabets   END.

Akshat Khare

The Taste of Limes

O F the five taste modalities once available to man only three remain. There is much debate between men of science and phenomenologists if the other two really did exist. And if they did, what purpose they would serve.

The third cataclysm had taken with it much of the literature that once existed in the libraries that dot the map of our world. In the sources that remain, there are enough references across various languages and cultures about the five modalities with the missing sweet and sour completing the set.

The chief reason he believed it himself was the short but rich account found in the lower reaches of cascaria—the pages were from the journal of a monk who had lived during the time of the cataclysm.

The monk writes of a great unseen evil that swept the land and the hero who took up arms against it. The evil was from a different world and had slipped into ours through no fault of its own. But its confusion meant an end for all life if it in turn was not ended first. Ending it however, was no easy task. The vague enemy crept through the city unseen and unheard—the only indications of its presence were the bodies it left behind.

To wipe the nebulous or perhaps permeating enemy, the hero entered the realm of essentials. This was the only way to end the peril at its root, its essence wiped out for all time and all space.

The hero came across the essences of various entities and ideas, understanding things that had always seemed out of grasp in the waking world. He found the bright monads of truth, beauty, and justice. He turned his head and could see envy simmering in a corner, rage seething, avarice dripping, lust lurking and sloth crawling. He moved ahead and came across cruelty and apathy, and these too he left alone.

Finally, he came to that corner of the realm where the numinous existence of the peril dwelled. Its corruption had begun to spread to this world as well. The destroyed essences of unknowable ideas were already in its tendrils. The peril had entrenched itself in the sweetest sweet and the sourest sour and it could not be ended without also ending the others. The hero hesitated, but then he saw the tendrils of the peril shivering out of a giddy delight and creeping out to the other nebulous entities around it. And so, having resolved himself, he swung his blade. The metal had not even made its way completely across before tangerines began to shrivel up and fall from their trees. Mangoes and Apples all began to die off at once and people around the world started forgetting not just about the peril but also about these two tastes they had long cherished.

The monk who raised lime trees and orange trees in his garden saw the oranges shrivel up and having intuited what had happened rushed to his table to write about the taste of oranges. But found himself unable to do so.

The limes remained with him because they were not just sweet or sour but chiefly and often; bitter. So, the monk sat down and started writing what he could of the taste of limes.

Kent Kosack

Formula for Elephants

Because she called and said come to Brooklyn, I was in a warehouse in that hip borough sitting on a metal folding chair with a damaged leg causing it to list sideways as a bodybuilder who went by the stage name "Elephantis" performed naked kendo kata with a stiff neon purple pool noodle and an equally stiff eleven-inch cock. I couldn't squirm in my chair because, again, the listing, and if I shifted even in the slightest, I would have slid off and landed with a thud in the aisle and for some reason I knew that Elephantis would come to my aid and with his twenty-inch biceps deadlift me into the sky and I didn't want to ruin, or become part of, his performance.

My friend had told me she was performing and that was all. I recalled her growly "Lean on Me" solo in our sixth-grade choir class and imagined something along those lines. Innocence and harmony with a smidgen of playful grit. Instead, I had Elephantis as the centerpiece to some sort of indie erotica vaudevillian circus. After him, a nude acapella group sang bawdy doowop succeeded by a hypnotist who led a woman from the audience to believe she was being strangled. While hypnotized, mid-strangulation, she orgasmed violently on stage, toes curling like the talons of a raptor seizing its prey. Once the hardworking custodian did his best to sanitize the stage, my friend made her entrance wearing black loafers with large metal buckles catching the light, an odd venue to see shoes that I associated with children wearing while playing Pilgrims in Thanksgiving plays. She wore these loafers and only these loafers.

The audience was quiet enough that we could hear the squeak of her soles across the stage and the creak of the wheels of the cart of sex toys she pushed before her. I wasn't present. I felt a distance there, in the dark, in the quiet of that dark warehouse in that foreign borough, breathing the breaths of sixty-odd strangers and watching a person I thought I knew—the girl on roller-skates gamboling up my driveway, the teen rolling joints beneath our high school bleachers—now with a look on her face I couldn't place, half-pain, half-glee, while she electrocuted herself. This woman's skin reddened and bruised and it wasn't the pain that surprised me or whatever it was inside her that drew her to it, that sought it out. It was that I didn't know her. I didn't know maybe the only person I thought I knew. Who was she? What moved her? What brought her joy? I had no idea what her life was like, all of the little moments that accumulate to constitute a life. I only knew the scraps of information she threw me: one adventure here; a fuck there; a book she enjoyed last year. But did I know her, this woman, naked and in pleasurable pain performing on a stage in a warehouse in Brooklyn?

I left before her finale. But, given her ecstasy and my discretion, I doubt she noticed.

My friend and I had been meeting up quarterly since we'd graduated high school. For a decade I'd trekked out to see her in a dorm in Burlington or a loft in Philly or a cabin in the Berkshires, wherever she was currently holed up. Or, as if to confirm her memories of the place she'd rejected and the life it represented, she'd visit my mother and me. She'd tell us tales, regaling us with stories about interesting people in exotic places and exotic people in interesting places, while quietly disdaining our decision to waste our lives on this dull suburban New Jersey street. Now that my mom had no more life to waste, I took up the mantle of chief dullard when I inherited the house. And I enjoyed my new role as homeowner. I'd spent my twenties cautiously eyeing the ladder of adulthood when my mother's sudden death and my consequent inheritance—the deed to my childhood home, the home my friend had grown up down the street from—seemed to propel me to the highest wrung. From these lofty heights I watched my footloose friend change careers, cities, and lovers as often as I mowed the lawn. My home fit me. Or perhaps I'd grown to fit it. Either way, I became increasingly attracted to the rootedness the home provided and to the endless list of chores to maintain it that gave structure and meaning to my days.

It was here, in said home, where we next met, two months after her performance. She arrived with her usual knock despite the new doorbell I'd installed. I opened the door and she handed me an origami elephant.

"A souvenir," she said, pointing at the elephant now standing unsteadily in my left palm.

I inspected the little creature: crinkly paper ears, a sharp, pinched, paper trunk, and feeble-looking paper feet. Not exactly elephantine. Nor Elephantis.

"New landscaping?" she asked, pointing at the mums I planted on either side of the front steps.

"They're perennials if you tend to them right."

She pushed past me and my new paper elephant and surveyed the living room. "Rattan? Jesus."

"What's wrong with rattan?"

"This isn't a living room. It's a mausoleum outfitted with furniture from the 80s."

It's not a mausoleum. It's a Cape Cod with a new roof, a dry basement, and no mortgage." I followed her into the kitchen where she stood inspecting the framed photo of my mother atop the fridge.

"A shrine with tacky wallpaper."

"I am thinking of redecorating," I said, though I wasn't.

She shook her head at my mother's image and ran her fingers over the counter, then under it, as if she were trying to lift it. To topple it. I could see the strain in her forearms, like she was trying to overturn not just the counter but the whole house, me, the world.

I looked at the elephant in my hand and thought of the elephants in Africa hunted to near extinction for their ivory tusks to be turned into bangles, piano keys, and Japanese seals and how their children, too young to have valuable tusks, either died alone or were cared for in elephant orphanages where their handlers struggled to find the right formula to feed them. They tried a mix of everything: cream, butter, coconut milk. One version the elephants couldn't digest. Another wasn't substantial enough, wasn't nourishing, so the elephants slowly starved. They lost a lot of them over the years, but eventually they discovered the right recipe. And I thought about my friend's arsenal of sex toys and me listing in that metal chair. Thought of the mulch I laid over my wintering mums and the dirt laying over my mother.

"Are you staying for dinner?" I was hoping for a simple evening with a friend.

"Yes. I thought we could do a movie night. I brought something."

"What?" I went into the kitchen to start on dinner, chopping garlic and onions and putting water on to boil. It was Wednesday and Wednesday meant pasta night and leftovers for days. My linchpin, routine, midweek meal.

"A movie I made."

"You're a filmmaker now? What kind of movie?"

"Let's just watch it," she said, settling into the rattan armchair in the living room despite her previously voiced aversion.

"You won't tell me what kind of movie it is?"

She sighed, tapped her fingers on the rattan. "Well, you could call it a pornographic movie."

I stopped chopping. "Like an arthouse movie with a little nudity?"

"No. As in a movie where I'm fucking." She cocked her right eyebrow at me. "A lot. Pure, joyful, fucking."

"A little racy for Wednesday pasta night, no?"

"Afraid you'll choke on your penne?"

"Can't we just have a nice dinner and catch-up? Like two old friends." I returned to the familiar task before me and sliced another onion down the center, removed its papery skin.

"You are my friend, right?"

I nodded, still focused on the butcher block, the onion, the blade of the knife against my knuckle.

"So, aren't you interested in where I'm at right now? To see who I am?"

"I do. I want, I see." I did. And I didn't.

"Well, this is part of me right now and I'm actually really proud of it and want to show you, probably my oldest friend, what I've done. Is that not OK?"

I turned around and looked at her over my mother's linoleum counter. "I guess I don't want to see you exploited."

"No one was exploited. I wanted to do it and was paid. Paid well, in fact."

"Prostitutes are paid but that doesn't mean they're not exploited." I knew I'd said the wrong thing. I returned to my chopping. I was through my second onion at that point. My eyes were tearing up but I kept at it.

"You know, sometimes I don't know why I bother with you. Why I keep coming back here. You're so fucking static." The rattan creaked again as she stood. She brought the movie to the kitchen, a small black DVD case, and left it on the counter. "In case you decide you give a shit." And she left.

I ate the pasta by myself. It was more slimy onion than sauce but I had my routine and refused to let her latest whim derail it. Yet I watched the movie. The film. Whatever you call it. I watched it through twice. It was good, whatever that means for porn. Well-lit. Well-acted. She looked incredibly self-possessed. Fucking, being fucked, whichever, both. She was savoring it, the camera, her body, the erotic performance of herself, of a self. I imagined myself as the cameraman hovering nearby, zooming in, trying to capture parts of her, then all of her, then parts again. Not a creep or a voyeur but a professional trying and failing to find the right frame.

I DIDN'T HEAR from her until the following summer. She called from California where she'd finagled a gig as a farmer. She lived with a quiet family on a small organic farm and did quiet tasks. Hard tasks, but, she said, honest ones. Rejuvenating, rewarding work. Digging trenches and tilling the earth. Planting multi-colored carrots and resilient brassicas. Plus, some mail-order mushroom harvesting venture I couldn't quite understand. She said the nights were magnificent. She'd lie there, sleeping in a tent more often than not, breathing in the manure and rot giving way to new life, all wrought by her own dirty hands. Her legs grew hairy. Her two eyebrows merged into a single lustrous one.

I spoke with her twice during her bucolic period. She rambled through the first conversation, giddy with back-to-the-land fervor. The second conversation revealed a marked, but not unexpected, decline in her former exuberance. The work now sounded less invigorating than back-breaking.

"What have you been working with recently?" November had come to my patch of suburban New Jersey, cold and crisp. But California was an unknown country.

"Vegetables," she said flatly. "Rutabagas or some shit. I don't know."

"And are you staying on for the winter? Is there stuff to do?"

"There's always stuff to do. Animals to tend. Crops to harvest or water or plant. Fences to mend. There's never not stuff to do."

"Sorry. I have no idea what happens on farm. I'm a suburban creature."

"You have no idea of anything, really. You've never been anywhere or done anything."

I didn't know how to take that. While it was true that I was no globetrotter, I did a lot every day. I woke up. I drank coffee. I ran. Did laundry. Worked. And I went places. To the grocery store. The park. On occasion, even a museum or the movies.

"Listen, I'm just a little tired is all. The rainy season is coming and I'm just tired. But hey, I've met someone."

"Tom Joad?"

"Whose chode?"

"Never mind."

"He's from Chile. He's working on the farm for the fall then bumming around California a bit, you know, San Francisco, Alcatraz, Universal Studios. Then he's going back to Santiago. It's spring there now. He'll get two summers."

I could tell where she was going but asked anyway. "And you want to go with him?"

"I don't know. I'm getting a little tired of being isolated here. The monotony, you know? Oh, I suppose you don't." She laughed. "But he's super cute and bright. He's a poet. Writes a lot about flowers and dictatorships."

And he did, of course, invite her. I received a package from her just before Christmas. Inside, a folded piece of lined paper with a brief, exclamatory note on the back:

Hey, friend! How's the homestead? The mums?

I'm going to Chile! Going to learn Spanish and drink wine and climb mountains. Not sure if your green thumb has any experience with fungi but here's a little something to let you try your hand at it. See you when I see you.

Enclosed with the note was a plastic bag with a large, gray hunk of wood in it. A log for mushroom farming with simple directions. An idiot-proof way to harvest your own fresh mushrooms in your home, it said. I followed the directions, watering the rotting log in a giant enameled canning pot in my basement. It stank like a mildewing sock. After three weeks, instead of dozens of little shitake mushrooms, I proved myself an idiot and got one huge, spongy phallus. I threw the log in the backyard by the shed to see if anything else would grow on it in the spring. Nothing did.

I saw HER the following summer in my kitchen again, much thinner, but I couldn't tell if it was the result of healthy living or the opposite. She brought back yerba mate and special cups and straws to drink it, and a bottle of pisco which she opened the moment it came out of the bag, in almost one motion. Here it is, there it goes.

I put the electric kettle on for the mate but she filled two cups with pisco and handed me one after downing half of hers. I figured it was the opposite.

So, Chile?"

"Did I tell you about the sunsets on the farm in California? They were different, I swear. More golden, cleaner, less red. With the smell of the wet earth. The sun feels fatter there. A flower in full bloom."

"Very poetic. And how were the sunsets in Chile?"

"I don't remember."

"You back for a visit or for good?"

"I don't know." She looked disappointed. With me or herself, with her story or the world's, I couldn't tell. "I'm here, yes, and going, and back. Good, I'm not so sure. But you look good and you're still here. This house is still here," she said, tapping the bottom of her glass on the counter. "Yes. I always come back. Sometimes with souvenirs, sometimes not. You like the pisco?"

I nodded, feigned another sip. "But what happened to the farmer poet? Your romantic novio?" I remembered the word from high school Spanish. It sounded both new and negative.

"He was nice too."

"But you're here and he's not."

"You're very observant." She poured herself another pisco and raised her glass to the photo of my mother on the fridge.

"So, what happened?"

"It's what didn't happen that happened."

"Is that a riddle?"

"I had a miscarriage."

"I'm sorry. I didn't know you'd been pregnant." I didn't know how to respond. I didn't know a lot of things about her. I knew that much.

"I didn't plan on it. I thought about coming home for an abortion. My abortion vacation." She laughed. "But I warmed to the idea. To bringing a life into this world. To have a little someone to share it with."

"I'm sorry."

"You could have been her uncle. Uncle Pasta Nights. The uncle with the tacky wallpaper and the mums."

"I would have liked that."

"Did I send you any of his poems? My novio. I was mad about his poetry."

"No, I don't think so."

"It doesn't matter. I didn't really understand them anyway. My Spanish sucks."

SIX MONTHS LATER I received a postcard from Mt. Marcy in the Adirondacks. She was finishing up a meditation retreat at a

Zen monastery in the mountains there. The picture on the postcard was a close-up of green and orange lichen on a pile of gray rocks, life growing on rubble. On the back she'd simply written "Thinking of you" followed by her name. Two weeks later she was on my front porch doing origami. I pulled up and there she was, surrounded by paper animals, sharply-folded rabbits, deer, and elephants. A Saint Francis of origami.

"You have enough for an origami zoo."

She smiled. We went inside, leaving the paper menagerie on the porch, trembling in the wind.

"Is the tree still falling in the wood?"

"Can I have a beer?"

She maintained eye contact longer than I was comfortable with. I opened two beers and offered her one but she didn't take it.

"Can you put them down for a second?"

"Sure." I put them on the counter, one on each side of the sink.

"Can I hug you?"

I nodded. She came over and hugged me, held is more accurate, for several minutes. It felt awkward at first, or at least I did. But once I stopped thinking it became nice.

"Thanks," she said, releasing me and stepping back slightly though still firmly in my personal space. "I'm sorry about how I've treated you. Dumping my shit in your lap. The show in Brooklyn. My movie. The baggage from Chile. It's not fair."

"No problem. We're friends, right?'

She held my gaze for a moment more, then nodded. "Let me have that beer."

We took our beers to the porch. She talked about the monastery and meditation and silence and the cold morning mountain air and how up high it felt like another season and the muffled sounds of the monks' feet thudding along the wooden floors during walking meditation and the spindly, windswept pines growing out of cracks in the rockface at tortured angles trying to reach the sun and the quiet of the place pouring into her. How porous she felt. How calm. And I told her about using my mother's key to enter my home for the first time as her body lay cooling in the morgue. My shock at how a home so full of memories could feel so empty.

Our conversation felt, finally, comfortable. Felt real. None of her disdain, none of my distrust.

Later on, once our fingers were numb from the cold, we warmed up by walking around the old neighborhood, past the ranches and vinyl-sided split-levels and brick colonials, the blue light of television screens flashing out of the windows and briefly casting silhouettes of ornamental shrubs—leafless Japanese maples and dead-headed hydrangeas—across empty lawns. We returned to my porch and she tried to teach me how to meditate. But I'd had too many beers. I fell over a dozen times and couldn't uncross my legs to get up. We laughed about how inflexible I was.

"I like it here," she said, running her hands along the wooden floor of the porch as we listened to the sporadic sounds of the suburbs. A child shrieking in fear or delight. A car starting. Garages doors opening, closing. The slap of a skateboard hitting pavement.

"Me too."

"I can see why you never left."

"I didn't really have a choice. It was left to me."

"Everyone has a choice. But you chose to tend your own garden. Live in your place, in your way. I admire that. Though I never said so."

"And I admire how adventurous you are. How you're open to new experiences, how you seek them out. Your courage. Though I never said so."

"It's not courage," she said.

"Trying new things is courageous."

"It's not courage," she repeated.

"What is it, then?"

She took a deep breath and looked around. "Can I stay here tonight?"

"Sure. You don't have to ask."

"Thanks."

We went inside. I made up the couch for her and, since she had no extra clothes, I lent her my mother's flannel nightgown. She smiled and we said goodnight.

Twenty minutes later, she knocked on my door. "Can I sleep in here?"

"Is the couch uncomfortable?" I had a guestroom but she always preferred the couch. I didn't know what else to say or offer.

"No. It's just, I don't know. I think I want to sleep in here tonight. If it's OK."

"Sure." But I didn't sound sure. My throat was dry. I became very conscious of my bed, how small it seemed—my mother's queen, but suddenly it shrank to the size of the single I'd grown up with.

I scooched over to cede her some space. She sat on the edge of the bed, undid my mother's nightgown, folded it, and placed it on the armchair beside the bed. Out of the corner of my eye I looked at her shoulder blades, at the knobs of her spine, at the tightness of her skin. I had seen her naked before—on stage and on screen—but never like this. She wasn't sexy or sexual or sexualized. She wasn't performing. She was vulnerable. Present and real, of the world and in it. One frail body in a big, fraught world. Two, if you counted me beside her. Though at that moment the world didn't seem so big.

She slid under the covers and spooned me. I felt her breasts through the back of my tank top and her breath on my neck. Her hands were cold but I felt hot, feverish. I started to remember her video, the creak of that cart she pushed on stage, my mother, the strange antiseptic smell of her hospice, the way her doctor's explanations sounded more like condescension than compassion. The lusterless hospital lights. The emptiness of my old home newly mine. I started to cry even though I hadn't shed a tear at the funeral. To cry and then sob. And I kept sobbing while my friend held me and breathed on my neck until I fell asleep.

I woke up alone. I put on my usual sweatpants and robe and went to the kitchen to start my day. I looked outside at my neighbor's fence and thought of the grass in the summer when it grows too long and how some mornings I'd see flattened patches from where deer had lain. If I was up early enough, I'd see the deer, quick and light, slipping through the woods to take their chances crossing New Jersey's congested and manic maze of parkways and turnpikes. On such days I often envied the deer their swiftness, their ability to make any grass their home. Later, I'd wonder if I'd see a fresh carcass on the highway on the way to work.

On the kitchen counter I found a pile of origami paper. The same paper she'd used, but unfolded. The animals were gone, reverted back to blank pages. All that remained were the creases she'd made.

Ben Libman

Will the Circle Be Unbroken

And it is—yes just as the man said, over by the foot of the massif just north of here, northeast, Owens Valley well below, that must be what it is, lake the color of opal, she would have wanted to see behind her glasses, but the sun is low now time to set camp, nevermind the hole in the tarp, nevermind patching it up, haven't the energy, my damned knee, all this in endless returns, "my damned knee," thinking it but really we are talking you and I, really I am trying to tell you something like the wind, like I was back in the country, like I knew she was dying, it was a matter of time, knew it from the minute I got there, knew it from the minute I picked her up at the train station, like she was still beautiful, still un-twisted, was still more beautiful than I could handle but she had death on her, death stuck to her time, don't know how I knew, she had a hat, I still remember, a hat with a little feather in it, "a smart hat," she wore the hat and a pair of dark glasses for the ride, and I was so happy to see her, I was so happy to see her in her smart hat and dark glasses, a hat and glasses and a silk dress, I remembered her so small just looking at her, she had waited and waited, it was love, even death, right then I knew, I swear I knew, I knew, the hat had a little green feather which she swirled around in a circle and the feather became a circle an oval an ichthus, yes, ichthus and the fish was everywhere, oh yes, the fish with scales and its insides hanging out, the fish which is a fish with sharp teeth, a primordial fish, a fish that eats you, a fish that eats your nails, but I'm not going to tell

you that, I'm not going to tell you about my hand, I'm not going to tell you about the river the river that flows from the mountain, northern folk, southern folk, the river, the river, the river, the river, that's what I'm try-ing to tell you about, how the river flows from the mountain, the river which is the river, the river that leaves the mountain and flows into the desert, the river which is a river, the river which is a mountain, the mountain which is a mountain, the moun-tain which is a river, the river which is a mountain, the mountain which is, well, what is it exactly, up over the ridge-line now and how does it plunge sharply like that, all the way down like that?, man in a blue broad-brimmed hat on the path down below there, but how or where?, but oh, oh no drop at all, oh an illusion, oh oh the light upon that small puddle there, I thought it went all the way down somewhere, I thought it was more than myself and this angle, I lay that night with my eyes open and I saw the sky, I lay that night with my eyes open and I saw the sky and I saw the stars, I lay that night with my eyes open and I saw the sky and I saw the stars and I saw the little green fish with scales and its insides hanging out, I lay that night with my eyes open and I saw the sky and, careful not to trip here but this bit of flat granite will do, this bit and I can stretch out just fine, can string the tarp from this tree to the other and sleep right on the granite in my bag, and it's true what they say about the sky high up here being so dark during the day, almost black during the day, the granite being the brighter, and the night blinding by contrast with stars or swollen moon (none tonight that I can see), shall I or shall I not?, a blister to be popped, rather keep it intact lest the fluid, or, yes, keep it in-tact, when I press it gives soft and fleshy like the belly of a fish, could grab that bit of obsidian over there and just slice into it, piles of it just down a few steps I can tell, traps the stars down below here atop the granite, old knapping site Old Indians, five thousand years or more, seven thousand years at least, come through the valleys along the divide over there, "over yonder," commune of tribes trading tipping stout wooden mugs to their lips singing "yes, oh yes," knapping down there surely, up here too though why I don't know, or to what purpose I mean, if you were here you'd stop me rambling, stop me spilling my words like guts, if you were yes, unbearably loud in here in this skull here, more so than if I were to shout over this canyon, if you were pinned like a daemon to the top of that massif would you hear it?, if yes then this yes too, I'd say, I used think about what movie star I was going to be most like when I grew up, how I was going to be, who I'm going to be all angry and mysterious like Dirk Bogarde, machismo and passion like Alain Delon, who I'll be like, who'll be a writer like me? who'll be a simple guy like me? who'll be a boy like me? who'll be a man like me? who'll be an artist like me? who's going to be a writer like me?, who's going to have a green card like me?, who's going to be an American like me?, who's going to be an American who looks like me? I ought to shut up and make this lasagna, astronaut food you know, ultralite like that man I passed who clipped my shoulder with his fast-running elbows, I smelled his sweat and we shared a little bit of something, a little bit of the end of the curl of a lip, or something, a little something you share when there's no time to meet like humans meet, faint lines that no god would see cross, no matter would care an electron about, or something, a little something and but that man stopped

four maybe five or six feet later, after the crossing I mean, didn't call to me didn't have to, I just heard him stop, interruption of silence, heard him stop or turn and so I turned as if at a question, his still feet splayed, his feet a large question mark in the granite chips and parched debris, said old man you sure you want to go that way? and yes I said why not, why shouldn't I, suppose he was being polite, shrugged all polite as if to say my mistake but what he said was long pass, snail-like all the way around the pluton, word I'd never heard pluton, word like a scientist in a cartoon about the future of human beings and human fish, snail-like all that way, yes when he said "snail" like that I thought only of the brown garlicky cooked ones you never could eat, can you now? never could, do you now? never quite heard all of what he said as some wind passed between us at that moment, for some reason we didn't approach one another, some understanding it would be a regression, losing distance, so I said yes, oh yes, I'll be just fine, heading to the opal lake, the one shaped like an opal with the white creamy water, the one looking like an opal, the man with the elbow and sweat though just shook his head, no he said, no, he said, the lake wouldn't be reachable from there, it's not on the crest, it's by the massif over yonder, "over yonder," so not reachable unless I wanted to descend the pluton, "descend the pluton," the lunar module inserting itself as it did that one day, candy wrappers strewn on the ground before the sofa between Papa's feet, he hollering, blackwhite and grainy and some ill-understood words from the smudgy astronaut, as if a wind had passed through them, lunar wind like in some future universe of humans, and how long to descend the pluton I asked but basically shouted because of the wind, as I said, or thought, and he needn't have heard because he understood and said more than I could spare, maybe a joke, but yes now I see what he means it's there alright, opal and opal, granite, opal, valley, sublime triptych, so very far away it hangs like a Victorian mirror in space, like another planet bent oblong by something, I'll just go up and back, then, I said to him, I'll just go up and back, I'll just go up to the nearest peak and back, I'll just lay eyes on it, you know, from a distance and back again, and why he asked without asking (because of the wind), and why bother or something, and well there was no time to tell him of your obsession you earned from that book with glossy photographs, the book with glossy opal amethyst garnet emerald peridot lakes, obsession is it fair to call it an obsession? the kind of thing you might throw me a look for, but would you, then, throw me a look? one more time? behind all the space between, it doesn't matter, across all the time between us now, it doesn't matter, I could catch it, like hers behind her glasses, hers beneath her hat with the feather in it, anachronism like her death, that's what it is, and shall I tell you about that or the mountain, or down there the river and the folk who lived on either side of it, northern and southern, death we put right in their time, or the man with the elbow who thickened our crossed lines by stopping like a question mark, or the tarp which I should not have tied from this tree to the other, because when ever does it rain here?, and it not raining hardly ever, why would I block my view of the stars like that? of the extraplanetary opal spilling like that? of my baby like that? all I came up here to find, well from the top of a mountain like this you can see just about everything, no matter the distance between or the time between, could see you just about, could see your house a million miles away, with your yellowed windows in the night a million miles away and the hands slipped around your waist a million times telling you things I should've, hands that speak like elbows and sweat, gentle somehow and also taut somehow around your belly like a fish, intact like a fish with its guts and its wits still all there, yellowed window a million miles and flies vying to get in and your light-limited view of the opal necklace out there somewhere a billion million miles back toward the beginning, seven thousand years at least, seventy thousand years without a doubt, seven hundred thousand and there's no one here even to doubt, just this granite and this obsidian which wouldn't be here because it had to be brought, just this granite and this pluton and the opal lake and the valley, and some four-legged hind who wouldn't mistake the puddle for depth or a man in a blue hat, who looks up at the necklace and struggles to dream of the human future, of the cartoon scientist who will say "pluton," ichthyologist who'll say "platypus," and a great deal to be said for the opal isn't there? and more than just the opal, isn't there? and more than just the opal and the opal, isn't there? where did you learn to get obsessed like that? could you teach me to be obsessed like that? to cling to one thing like that? to love something like that? where did you learn not to wander and think you could get from the pluton to the spot beneath the massif no problem no matter what the elbow and the sweat told you, no matter the question mark in the granite dust? where did you learn lunar modules? where did you learn to lose distance? no fires up here though it would be a good beacon, but can't forget the lasagna, can't forget to cook the astronaut food, ultralite like him, a bit of water left in the bottle but not enough I think, could go back up to the puddle with the blue hat in it, could go back but lose distance, this'll do or it'll have to, a little boil over the little stove and a little splash in the astronaut pouch and then wait, then stare up but I should really take this tarp down, like sunglasses over the eyes of a lost daughter, and will it really come out a lasagna like that? square and broad-noodled like that? of course not but in the human future of cartoon scientists and cartoon ray guns and real-live food printers it will come out like that, square and broad-noodled like that, oh my knee, that was the moment, "oh my knee," Papa gripping his by the television set as the creamy astronaut spoke across the wind and the time, twisted it in the parched debris, twisted it when our lines resumed their crossing, thickened by that granite-mark and the elbow's warning and the pluton's descent, twisted like your unnatural mouth when I told you, like the wheel guard and the engine smoke and the redwhite feather from the hat and the sunglasses twisted around the bridge, and the arm up and behind and the legs vanished beneath the dash and the upper and the lower and the fire and the twain, and the look lost behind the glasses behind the eyes shut off like that old television being pulled from the edges to a single bright point, then off, pulled like the blood in your face pulled to the red point of your red tongue and the white of your shocked skin when I told you, and her life like the screen of the television when it happened, and the tarp now pulled from this tree and the other and the stars now, and my breath now being drawn and stretched sheet-like across all the in-between and everything pulled out to a point like the astronaut beyond the wind to a point like the opal on the ring of your hand holding the hand holding your fish belly in the yellow light of the fly-beloved window to a point, to a single point at the beginning of time in the human future.

Glenn Ingersoll

A Window

I stand with the blind before the window.
At the edge of every pane some sunlight pries.
When somebody sees us, how do we know?

In the way we stand, what do we show?
I don't want to be mean. Please think I'm nice!
I stand with the blind before the window.

I'm not sure I see, you see? But what do I know?
The fact is, the truth takes several tries.
When somebody sees us, how do we know?

I don't see everything. I don't want to.
What if we hurt them with our eyes?
I stand with the blind before the window.

When you don't know where to, where do you go?
They really are warning signs, these sighs.
When somebody sees us, how do we know?

The way he looks, that's where I'll go.
But how does he look? And is it wise?
I stand with the blind before the window.
When somebody sees us, how do we know?

If tragedy's intimate, comedy's distant.

Daniel Felsenthal

Six Poems

Midwestern Mean Time

After we dialed our
Clocks back to two,
Those subsequent dawns,
My mother pulled open
The blinds sharply, so sleep
Got black-bagged by the dark
Of winter, how static on a
TV seems disappeared by
Unknown operatives when you
Turn off a dusty Cathode set.

I grumbled, and somehow
She was charmed.
Sometimes, even, she got
Under the blanket with me,
Smelling sweatless elementary
School scalp before I brushed
My teeth and walked into a cold
That shook me awake, a father's
Ghost—Chicago, I once thought,
Was actually my dad.

Now that I am older, everyone accepts:
Only two seasons truly exist,
Summer and winter. During each,
I sleep in the daytime, curtains open,
Basking in the sun, soaking up the
Penumbra, covers thrown, naked,
Confident I won't be murdered,
become a tax lawyer, an athlete, a plain
Dweller. My sweat,
Matted into the mattress:
Rorschach Blots inked in sepia.
While I slumber,
I am drunk and famous.

Every year, across this city,
And New York, and Montreal,
And Toronto, and Berlin,
People try to hook up before
The long season. Not picky,
They just have to warm mutual bones

While waiting for the sun to shine.
Last October my friend went
On a Tinder date with a celebrity,
A rich film and TV star
With a certain (Oh, what's the
Expression?) *noblesse oblige*,
And evidence of being
Surprisingly well-versed
In the splashiest depths
Of contemporary
Literary novels. It's funny
How we make excuses
For people with a staff
To do so for them. "Blame
A guy with 738k followers
Because he's slow to respond?"
My friend asked. "Just because
You're a company
Doesn't mean you
Don't have needs."

I wish ill
Health on famous
People, and a hearty
"Don't care"
For their fans.

This new year, I hope to say
"I love you" to someone
And mean its opposite—
A serene, unpanicked
Disinterest. To be
Breezy, and easy,
With a warmth, rising,
Confident in its glow,
Only to set so quickly,
It's as if Daylight
Savings time just ended,
And love is a stolen hour
He stores in his nest
For fallow months.

To Be Born, But Actually, After the 1960s Lost Their Wind

While lust pulls us
Out of our rhythm
We realize the people
We pine for might only
Be good in the abstract.

One way to find out.

Sadly, solely someone a
Half century older than I am,
Like the men I think attractive,
Could find my
Predicament anything
Other than predictable—
Could deem my poesy
Profound.

Been there, done that.

Their belief: In free
Love. It fades.
if not from money, then
At the same pace
As their lives negotiate
Death. Treat every
Night like a last chance.

Not mine, for I never
Had a first chance.

Now That I'm Older

Morning dreams
Of a swollen hour
What'd you smoke,
Who'd you do?
Time as a unit of distance,
In which it is
In so many ways, used.
Walk cul-de-sacs
Just to stay still, energetically:

Bar with light slatted
Through door
Sun hiding behind
So much blue
Bed risen with sound:

Last night's snack
Is still being enjoyed
Somewhere
In your body.

Drunk went from childhood prophecy
To grown-up feeling

All before you opened
Your right eye.
That one's tough,
Often crusty.

Mornings should have
No consequences
For being.

Just be. Remember
Who we are:
        Artists
Sleeper cells in
Restless times
Plotting revolution
Between our exposed
shoulder's cold
And the arms we

Hang over our bedsides
To check
Our phones.

Awakenings are called rude
For a reason.

Was I? Let me think:
    Honest
At best, but know
It was not about you. Never you.
When I stand, it's two.
I'm one again.
Doo-da-doo.

So much blue
That while sleeping was
Like all the tea in China!
Or Oil in Arabia
Has become rare
Today and to waste it on another metaphor
Would be villainous. Nostalgically so.

Slide from sheets, the sky gray.
Funny thing about
Vampirism is while the world gets older
You stay the same age.

The Gay Science

In flesh, on skin
Brief glimpses of
primordial matter.

In mottles, swirls,
Deep space pallor,
Capillaries burst
With starstuff. Like
War, the Big Bang
Never ended though
In this case we can't
Remember the start.
Carbon's diaspora
Hangs our wrinkles
& spreads our thighs.

All traumas are un-
Original, birth too,
Echoing, in world's
Ears, the singularity.

Nearer to space
Time's blow-up than
Minds, bodies store pain
Of refugees. For even simple
Organisms have billowing forms
While eggheaded H. Sapiens Sapiens
Have hard cerebrums we love to rely on.
Prehistoric physical memories make entrails
Churn, the lymphatic nodes in groins swell up, my
Eyes turn blurry & dry from reading about the war in
bed while you sleep & I contemplate your cheek's nebula,
the quantum oscillations of my waistline & how such obvious
Metaphors are naked and shameless so one can expand them endlessly
Until we have a whole skein of beliefs: why art has the form of the cosmos.

I won't, but I want to wake you
In order to speak & set you free:
The history of the spheres spins
In your breast, merely consider
The red herring in evolution's
Tale, how males have nipples,
Which science has explained
But for the same reason your
Doctor doesn't know what a
Rim job is failed to understand.
We don't wear dead ends but
Keys to open primeval gates.
Sex is a query, not a solution.

In other homes, atheistic str8s
Who are nonetheless, vessels,
Tell their children the galaxy
bears likeness to spilled milk.

Kiddos stare at candy wrappers
As if accidents of the heavens
reflect the way they had never

Chosen to live.

How Jesus Was And What It Has to Do With Me

Jesus had a curved spine, flat
Feet, chronic bowel problems
And a tendency to develop ulcers.
Not many people know about
His obesity, pre-diabetes, and
Hairy hole, his love handles
And big tits with staticky fuzz
Around the nipples. After all,
The zealots wrote his corp-
ulence out of history, and now,
Twenty thousand skinny, erect,
Baby-smooth statues are sold in
Sleepy bodegas and airy markets,
Smattering shelves by the boxes of
Rice-A-Roni, Tootsie Pops, Kraft Mac,
Matchbox cars, Ultralamb, Her Pleasure,
Blue Boy, Bolt, Double Bubble,
Lighters the deli guys use,
Last-all-night supplements,
And the candles of saints.

Jesus' spine was the only
Deferential part about him—
Except with you-know-who.
The Bible never mentions
Christ's junk, though
Even heathens will not be
Surprised to hear that he was
Circumcised. Very few people,
However, know that he was the first
Recorded person to hang weights
From his cockskin, an unusual
Merging of man and invention, like
Da Vinci and flight, or Edison
And sound.

Innovating the hooding of the
Head, Christ tried to reclaim
The magic of his immaculate birth.
Such an event was so central in his mind,
That he refused to be in the very room
When Mary was in labor with their firstborn.
The family Christ: erased from history.
He and Mary agreed—keep the boys uncut.
And while reasons for so much doctoring

Are historically varied, Jesus hated himself
For being born Jewish,
The writing of one harem reported.
They would know, after all:
Closet cases love to haunt brothels
Feigning their own mystique behind
Opaque personalities, worrying
About the venereal diseases that ravage
Their era, while hardly being able to hide
The jealousy they feel for the lovers
They ashamedly hired. What sex worker
Has time to put up with such fuckin' guilt?

And if you don't believe me that harems
Had scribes, well: Mary published
A popular pillow book, shared often
Among the alternative thinkers of
Galilee and Jerusalem and Damascus.
She was elderly when the memoir came out,
Beautiful, sun-drenched and covered with
Age spots, and Paul was one of her only
Old customers who was still alive. She never
Liked him. She had always refused him unlike
The other apostles, he was a crotchety crone
When he was young. And in his dotage
His nose had begun to run constantly,
Food and wine clung to his breath, and he had
Become hard of hearing, with cataracts clouding
His vision. His patience, which he had already
Strained to a quivering line, snapped somewhere
Along, well—um—I guess, along the "line."
He was crazy and megalomaniacal:
His grown children wouldn't even let him
See the grandkids.

Sometimes I offer services
To older men with children
Who don't speak to them.
They talk to me about their
Wayward boys. I love these
Men instead of my own dad,
Which is a funny feeling.
Your body begins to float,
Like it would in the dead sea,
And you settle into yourself.
Less futile than blame, prayer,
Or forgiveness.

Every time I meet a new daddy
I wonder if he will be a Paul type,
Someone who would burn a book
Just to quash the claims of a Mary:
For instance, that fathers
Do not deserve to be honored or adored
When they abandon, abuse and delude
Their sons, who anyway happen to be
33 years old.

But instead of lingering on speculation,
I buy my Blue Boy, and my pre-roll, and
Two Blow-Pops: Cherry and Sour Apple.
I thank the lady behind the counter,
Leaving the fleshless Jesus statues
To history, and its vivid excuse for
An imagination.

Lemon Party

Mornings when grandpa shat himself,
Nurse came to help grandma wipe.
Old hands just didn't work anymore.
While you lived beneath her nightie,
Other kids crawled through the window
No drapes would conceal again. Not even
Those that matched the motel carpets.

Your family's place, it was proudly
Sealed. Eight deadbolts. Solid brass
Chain and a rusted-shut gate
To the mossy fire escape. The
Glass decorating your door was
Plastered over. Scared fathers
And pharmaceutical victims robbed
Clueless ancestors when you were
A glint in that aluminum siding
The city would later tear down.

After the sun set, Christmas
Lights over lawns, they meant:
"Residents are home."

Saturdays, youth's pageant passed
By the foyer. Queen-waving, atwirl
Astride floats. But not a spot for you.
Ain't / no / window / wide / enough.
You had an alphabetized record
Collection, true, and books shelved
By subject (A-Z), a whole display of Yale
And Schlage locks ready to be spread
Like a suitcase of guns, in one
Of those movies you watched close
To the snowy pixels each night.

Through the haze of your comfort
You saw the wall's plaster peel
And crack. Maybe—you helped.
When a hole finally formed, through
The insulation and the drywall, it was
Too narrow to reveal the procession
That had always passed by your door.
You perched with your face up close:

First, there was a street, shown on
Cam. Green-grey, as if seen with
Night goggles, a man shoved his soft,
Small member, flesh unrolled like a map
Of boils and moles. There was an Arab strap,
In the grim, anti-Cubist pixels of a slow-loading
Internet stream. Busy hotel party furniture,
Every inch covered in hanging chicken legs.

To begin having sex so late can be hopeful
And also an act of will that forces you through
A crumbling oasis and into the violent sun.

Hands will pull at your pant
Legs. Kick family back inside.

And then push, hard now,
Treat the bodies of the dead
As springboards for the
Rest of your life.

NICK HOLDSTOCK

ADULTS

THREE men sat in an Indian restaurant with a nine-year old named Lucy. Mark, her father, had just finished praising her mental arithmetic, which he said was the best in her class. Ian said, 'That's great,' then took out his phone. He showed Mark a picture of a boy with a wide face and a bloated stomach. In another photo what looked like a different child was standing by a wall with one hand over his face. 'Johnny is discovering so many things,' said Ian with a pride he tried to make contagious. Steven, who was meeting Ian for the first time, did not ask to see the photos. He was cracking his poppadom but not eating it because in India they crumbled it into the rice. He was sure the other two adults would comment on this and had prepared an explanation. Neither Steven, nor the other two adults, noticed the look of wonder on Lucy's face as she sipped her mango lassi. It was the brightest, most intense flavour she had ever tasted. Behind her eyes, in the childish dark, a new sun began to rise.

'Steve, do you have kids?' asked Ian, who shortened people's names because he thought it was friendly.

'I really hope not,' said Steven, while laughing, and when Ian didn't even smile, he realised he had been too honest. A little fire of panic started but was quickly doused. This was the first remark Ian had addressed to him since they'd met. The guy had made no effort. Someone who couldn't even trot out *What do you do?* or *Are you from here?* was too narcissistic for him to care about. Steven was more concerned that Mark, his actual friend, might disapprove, but he didn't seem to have heard. Mark was correcting Lucy's posture, because she was slouching, though Steven suspected it wasn't her fault. The

chair was very slippery, and her feet didn't touch the floor, but he wasn't going to defend her. She was not his problem. Lucy didn't seem bothered by her father's half-jokey explanations about why it really mattered to sit up straight because otherwise she'd be a hunchback and have to live in a tower and in a tower there weren't any sweets. 'Yes, Daddy,' she replied while solar flares illuminated rooms in her skull she hadn't known existed.

Ian looked at several more pictures of his son. Johnny by the pond. Johnny with some crisps. Johnny reading a book and refusing to look up for the camera. Ian loved being a father: it was the best thing that had ever happened to him. But the world was full of haters like Steve who had no idea that their emotional spectrum was lacking the special, vivid colours only perceived by parents. Steve probably thought having a child was like acquiring a very demanding pet that would probably outlive its owner. He wouldn't understand the incredible bravery and mental strength it took to be responsible for an entity that was never going to be perfect. All Johnny's failings would be blamed on him and Paula, even stuff that was completely genetic, like his bloated belly and the terrible flatulence that often ruined meals.

'The worst thing about Brexit,' said Mark, deliberately raising his voice, 'is that even now there are still people making excuses for Leave voters.'

He glanced around the almost-empty restaurant, hoping to see an angry Brexiter because what could they do? They couldn't win the argument.

'All that crap about Leavers not having much education and being from deprived areas with high unemployment and needing to blame someone else instead of the Tory governments they've voted for. Essentially, you know, letting them off the hook completely and saying "It's not their fault", when, I'm sorry, it totally is. They have decided to make a bigoted, xenophobic decision based on fear and prejudice. Lou Lou, that's enough for now. Wait till the food comes.'

Lucy looked up from her half-empty glass. She licked the orange residue from her upper lip and waited for her father to get distracted. She was hopeful. He really liked to talk, especially to other men. It seemed to make no difference to him whether they were really interested.

'Anyway,' said her father and waited for one of the others to respond to his argument. But Ian was still looking at pictures of Johnny. Steven was crumbling his poppadom into even smaller pieces. It would be just like him to be sulking because Ian had been invited to their regular Friday lunch. It wouldn't have occurred to him that Mark didn't have much free time and so had no choice but to sometimes combine different friendship circles. That shouldn't be a problem. They were all adults. And yet he was obviously going to have to make Steven and Ian talk to each other.

'Steven, tell Ian what happened with your boss. Tell him about the email.'

Ian looked at Steven, then Steven looked at Mark, and as Steven felt a surge of annoyance at having to tell this embarrassing story to a stranger, Lucy realised that the raincloud of her father's attention had drifted away from her. She simultaneously brought down her head and raised the glass and then the sweetness returned to her mouth like a rush of sunlight through a gloomy valley. She wished she was home with the cat and a killer Sudoku. She didn't like curry. She wondered why her Dad was talking to these men he didn't like very much. Wasn't it like lying? Did he need attention that badly?

'I mean, we all make mistakes,' said Steven. 'It was partly my fault. I could have checked that our intern had uploaded the correct version of the article. She'd been doing a great job for the last three weeks, and so I totally trusted her. If that was wrong, I hold up my hand.'

Ian nodded in encouragement. He liked where this was going.

'But what I didn't expect was that I'd be blamed for everything. My boss sent me this horrible email in which she accused me of trying to destroy the company's reputation. It was just so unfair. All I'd done was cover for the intern and that was my reward. It's like I always say—no good deed goes unpunished.'

'Amen,' said Ian then worried that this made him sound religious. 'I totally agree. I think it's a common problem in management. So many people have all this power but no idea how to actually manage people. They expect everyone under them to be psychic. Last week my boss called me into her office and we had what I suspect she thought was a sensitive chat but which to me was really upsetting.'

'Oh yeah?' said Mark who suspected he was going to be subjected to a complain-a-thon. He glanced at Lucy, and when he saw she wasn't trying to drink her lassi, he was proud that she was being so good. Which she thought a little sad. Needing to take credit for his daughter's decision suggested he was as insecure as Ian, who was still complaining about his also female boss suggesting he work from home in order to deal with Johnny's medical issues. 'And you know what's really insulting?' Ian said and then their food arrived. His question hung in the air like one of Johnny's noxious emissions. Lucy watched the adults help themselves to whatever was nearest. They didn't pass anything. 'Just a little,' she said to her Dad but he nonetheless dropped a huge scoop of sag aloo onto her rice. Steven mixed his poppadom into his rice and got the reaction he wanted. He explained, in an offhand way, and Ian said, 'Great idea.' Steven was so grateful he said, 'What did your boss say that was so insulting?'

'Well, I don't want to make too much of it. It's just that she acted like she was doing me a favour. I'd rather she criticised me for taking time off than pretend she cared. It was so transparent. I mean, I want my rights as a father, but not if it means I get treated like an idiot.'

'Guys,' said Mark and they looked at him because he sounded very serious. 'Guys, I have to go to the toilet. Can you watch her please?'

'Sure,' said Ian, because for a competent parent it would be no problem. Once Mark was in the toilet he said to Lucy, 'What's your favourite thing here?'

'I don't like any of this,' she said. 'I don't like Indian food.'

'What do you like?'

'Everything else. But it's OK. Sometimes there are things you just have to accept.'

'Great,' he said and looked away. She was a strange kid. Smart, apparently a big reader, likely to grow up into someone popular and successful. Yet as Ian watched her sitting with great composure he suspected that in mid-life she would suffer a devastating crisis that would be far more traumatic and debilitating than it would be for an average person for whom failure, disappointment and rejection had been regular meals.

Lucy watched the two men shovel orange and green slop into their mouths as if they were buckets that had to be filled. Another heavenly gulp of her lassi made her vision go yellow, then white, then orange. Her mind was a high, wide plateau covered with wooden boxes that began to open with the confident elegance of flowers. From each box emerged a thought.

They're terrified.

They've no idea.

They cannot stop lying.

And then her Dad was back and his hands looked dry although he was supposed to wash them. He used those hands to tear off a piece of nan bread.

'What did I miss?' he said and tried to laugh but she could hear his worry that in his brief absence Ian and Steven had forged a new friendship from which he'd be excluded.

'I was just telling Ian about my plan to go to Uzbekistan next summer. I'm going for at least three weeks, and I'll write a travel piece, maybe a book. I don't think anyone's done that.'

She saw her father relax then prepare to assert his dominance. 'There's a reason for that. There's no market for that sort of thing. Obscure places are obscure for a reason and that's why they stay obscure.'

Her father's head contained a moth, a flickering bulb, centuries of dust that clogged every synapse. It was filthy. Disgusting.

'I hear what you're saying,' said Steven. 'The main thing is just to go and have a look.' Lucy was taken aback by the leaping flames of his anger at Mark's casual murder of his dream. Yet he did not feel able to publicly confront, let alone destroy, his old friend. But with a small surge of wonder Lucy realised that from this moment on Steven would be sharpening weapons. There would be sneak attacks, undercuts, faint praise in the peer group. Her father's social standing was sufficiently precarious—he was too successful; he lectured people; he could be a bully—that people would be glad to mentally unfriend him. Which would wound him. He would bleed. And so she had to warn him.

'Daddy, listen to me,' she said but he cut her off.

'Lou Lou, you have to eat something. If you don't, you can't have any more lassi.'

'Alright,' she said and took two big spoonfuls of rice.

'And not just rice. Have some spinach.'

He dropped a dollop onto her plate of a dark, oily paste-like substance that had been frozen, defrosted, drowned in ghee, reheated several times. All his favourite food was unhealthy. Her little heart was under attack from artisan pizzas and gourmet burgers and all the things he brought back from the farmers' market with the pride of the hunter. Even though he said he loved his Lou Lou, he was poisoning her.

She coated the nasty stuff with rice until she had a bolus that might have been just rice. She swallowed it with shame.

'Well done,' said her father with a conspicuous pride he aimed in Ian's direction.

'Johnny loves curry,' said Ian as if it proved his son's superiority. After Lucy had taken a merciful, permitted sip of her lassi, she understood that Ian was doing his best, really trying, but as a father, as a human being, he was going to fail. His good intentions and unsparing effort would not prevent poor Johnny from contracting his father's traumas, fears and limitations. His wife, whatever her good qualities, would be no vaccine. As for Steven, who was eating in contemptuous silence, he wasn't going to remain childless for long. His objections were not principled. He was simply scared.

'One more bite,' her father said.

She picked up the fork. She swallowed poison. *Never again*, she thought. No more would she allow him to think she was an extension of him.

'Good girl,' he said. 'Another thing you don't hear much about is how all these Leavers still rate European destinations as their favourite holiday spots.'

Lucy drained the glass of its incredible nectar. Her veins were full of yellow neon. She was incandescent. A final box offered its contents. She looked at her father, at his not-friends, saw only one solution.

She put her feet on the floor. Pushed back her chair.

'Honey, do you need the toilet?' said the man who was going to destroy her.

'No,' she said, to everything, and then began to run.

'Stop her,' Mark said to Steven, who quite rightly said, 'I can't.'

Then she was out the door. Running in summer warmth. She moved brilliantly fast, like light. Now there were no secrets. She understood it all. Within her pulsed an energy that must not be contained.

She dodged, weaved. There were shouts. They were coming for her but her little legs were a dynamo. The idiots had made this world but couldn't make her join it.

'Come on,' she said to two boys and hoped they understood. They were both eating chocolate bars, and perhaps some of their boxes were open, but obviously not enough.

She ran on, knowing there was nowhere to go. No escape. She'd run as long as she could.

MISSISSIPPI'S LOCATION NEVER CHANGES OVERNIGHT.

EXACTING CLAM

REYounG

Beauty

She walks in beauty, like the night
Of cloudless climes and starry skies;
And all that's best of dark and bright
Meet in her aspect and her eyes;

SHE WALKS IN SQUALOR, like the queen of night's hidden horrors exposed to daylight. Like something vile and monstrous arisen from a fetid swamp wherein are born the worst abominations of the sickest minds. To describe her is to name the unnamable, to speak the unspeakable, to mention the unmentionable, yay, to eff the ineffable. Her presence is like placing in the middle of a dinner table set for the politest of society a silver tray, a salver, upon which sits a steaming pile of turds garnished with wads of excrement-befouled toilet paper. She is to all eyes that look upon her and immediately wish they hadn't a gorgon, the Medusa. Her hair is a filthy fright wig, an outrageous Rastaman "do" that sticks out everywhere like paralytic snakes. At first glance she might be mistaken for a Taong Putik celebrant. Her face is a hideous plaster mask, a palimpsest of ancient applications of pancake, powder and rouge on top of naturally accruing sedimentary layers of city grime that do little to cover, disguise, indeed, that only serve to make more hideous the lumpkin potato nose, the tuberous and tumorous bumps and warts, the itinerant chin and mustache whiskers bristling like bergamot thorns. She is cocooned like some repugnant insect larva in filthy, archaeological layers of pants, skirts, sweaters, jackets, coats, socks, stockings, undergarments. And yet, before one actually sees her, is repulsed by, disgusted, *ugh*, what made me turn, look, *stare* at her, this *thing*, there is an underlying contradiction, a pheramonal force, a strange strong attractor, something like the place in the flower where the pollen resides for the honeybee, sweet nectar for the hummingbird, a sudden, intoxicating delirium that overwhelms one's senses, creates an immediate and insatiable desire, lust, craving in all, male, female and every variation on the gender spectrum regardless of age, young, old, infirm, barely sentient, or even religious vocation (priest, rabbi, imam, blushing novitiate). They all feel it, that urgent pull, like a fish tugging on the line or a divining rod diving down or in this case—*up*. Other animal species (because we too are—*animals*) respond to her, lift their noses, snouts, beaks, muzzles to the air, nod and bob and crane their necks in search of the source of this power, force, this *energy*. Even plants, flowers, vegetation, stamen and pistil, tender young twig and sprig strain toward her. She feels their eyes, their souls, their yearning petals fix upon her like heat-seeking missiles, and then the explosion in their brains, she feels it herself, *ka-boom*—like that, familiar by now, the shockwave of incomprehension, the disconnect between what they expect to see (a garden of earthly delights? a consortium of heavenly angels?) and what they actually see, and still that profound need to stare at, to confirm, pinpoint exactly what it is that they do see, this grotesque, this leprous, vile, repugnant, besmirched and befouled old hag, bag lady, crone, ogress, beldam no doubt escaped from bedlam. But, too late, already far, far too late to ever forget, to erase this image from their mind, to save themselves from the gorgon's lapidarian gaze, they avert their eyes in disgust, revulsion, *utter*, even as the first whiff *sniff?* tickles the ol' nasal factories, and then the deluge washes over them, floods, inundates the subterranean and cartilaginous catacombs of their sinus cavities, smothers, drowns, overwhelms their organs of smell, penetrates their brains like the distillation of an entire garbage truck-load of filth. For she smells even worse than she looks. She walks in a cloud of pestilence, noisome and foul, markets her own unique brand, curated, call it fragrance, perfume, shalimar, eau de toilet (no extra "t" and silent "e"), better said, eau d' morte, the stench of rot, decay, of hospital bedpans, of feces, urine, suppurating wounds, necrotic flesh, of old ladies' bloomerish underwear stained with runny diarrhea, the stale ale of dried urine, sweat, vaginal infections, dirty unwashed cunt, asshole. Foul beyond all understanding or knowledge of the word foul. The fetor of carcasses decomposing in the hot midday sun (don't ask what they're doing there), of rotten eggs, spoiled milk, rancid potatoes, pizza, broccoli quiche. She reeks like an outhouse in summer, like an open latrine stewing with unimaginable abominations of the alimentary process. No matter how you say it, yesterday, today and—it's a good bet—tomorrow, she stank, stinks, will have stunk. The stench slams into you, staggers you backward, clutching at your mouth, nose, throat like you've been blasted with poisonous gas. A young medical student (still can't get out of his mind that slip-up during the interview, why the fuck did he say *hypocritical* when he meant *Hippocratic?*) spots her and thinks of the wreckage of human flesh he had on the dissection table this morning, shouldn't have had that big country-style breakfast of eggs, bacon, home fries, grits and buttermilk biscuits before *urp*. The young beat cop and the young EMS driver are reminded of the street people they've attended to, digging their way through the folds of filth to give CPR, to plug hemorrhaging wounds, to spray or inject Naloxone, adrenaline, vital fluids. Move along, lady! the cop (Joey Malone, yeah, Nick's kid, nice boy, having a bad day) barks *German shepherd?* at her, disgusted, wincing, *ooooh, that smell*, even as he feels a conflicting urge *WTF?* stiffening in his pants and thinks, practically

shouts at himself in his head, You sick fucking pervert! The CEO talking on his cellphone doesn't see her, a chronic blind spot his ophthalmologist can never identify (*poverty*), but he sure as hell smells her. Sewers backing up again? Why doesn't John do something about it? That's why we put him in office, *The People's Mayor! Clean streets, not mean streets!* Oh, but it costs money, you know. *Taxes.* Oh no no no. She's in fragrant violation not only of civil and criminal law, statutes of morality, decency, etc. (blue nose, blue laws, right?), but the laws of nature. How can a human being look and smell so foul and still exist, not combust spontaneously, implode in a flaming miasma of noxious gases. One can imagine a diet selected from a menu of garbage pails, dumpsters, feral feline survival instincts, fish heads, moldy pizza (pepperoni), fermented Chinese take-out (spicy tofu stir fry), her body probably riddled with Sars, Corona virus, Ebola, tuberculosis, bubonic plague and who knows what other medical nightmares of the previous and current centuries. It's almost impossible to imagine there is sentience, a life and consciousness, inside this cocoon, chrysalis, mummy, also almost impossible *not* to imagine something tubular, squishy, yucky, a disgusting worm-thing, inchoate larva of a human clothes moth. (Has our traveler in the STC taken on a new role?) And yet, who would've guessed that in the eyes of this monstrosity, in her crystal orbs of sight, surprisingly *not* cloudy, cataractous, there gleams a brightness, starlight? Who would have suspected that inside this traveling horror show, this fetid corpse flower, putrefied rose, she feels pretty, oh, so pretty, pretty and witty and bright! She feels butterfly flitty, she feels ingenue innocent, she feels feminine and aery and light. She feels like—oh, I don't know—a fairy? She feels *magical*. And you know what, folks? She is.

Hélène Sanguinetti

"I took 3 cows to the countryside"

translated by Ann Cefola

I took 3 cows to the countryside
    Countryside leapt out my neck

3 real cows step outside the picture

.   .

Real dung topples out the sky,

.

.

.

Oh, new souls, says bird, to the scent, stunned
        endless turn around, all in wood nailed,
        (violet flies supervise)
        Brats hung on barbed wire, with a fond hoof
        you knock us over

NATURE I WANT ALL
TO DEVOUR NEVER
CONTENT WITH IT (encore)

For pancratium maritimum our delight,
For female bathers who chant males who swim to forget their name
Flakes of sea, of iron, of father in the closet, his comb, his teeth
that make you cry
continuing they freeze
all rise on the picture

.

.

.   Not yet
            noted

small plane
bottom shaven from field
Go above
study currents and corridors,
cast yourself away
the pure the other side

.   .

.

The path climbs right, not on the picture she
knows

.

Where are you midst those who speak and watch?   .

.

.

All words come to a stop
several on the edge with shovels
remains of foundation rubble
what for finally, you crazies in the ditch
of the desperate!
But barricade opens its arms
to illumine your way
Burst, Onyx heart!

GOOD BOOKS NEVER TURN BAD.

Oisín Breen

Five Poems

A Company of Remnants

Old fool me,
I stand here now,
Cutting back the hyacinth,
Waiting for the visitor
From yellow springs.

And I hear the wind,
And I watch drooping leaves
Turn heads,
Neatly pointing to the stars,
Carrying unspoken words.

Yet I cried this morning,
Into a cup, dense with remnants
Of loose leaf tea,
I cried for friends passed by
So quickly.

And their passing came so fast,
Faster than I knew it could,
Even though, when younger,
I argued youth's case,
Under the treacle dawn.

I argued
To any who would listen:
To rabbits,
Squirrels,
Even the wind.

But, even so, today, like all other days,
I tread the two steps down to the garden,
Outside my tired bungalow,
And I laugh,
Even though I long only for warmth.

Youth

when young,
I knew everything,
because I was everything.

at once quill, edge of sanity, loose-leaf
and coffee lovingly dripping black
on white,

white
on black

and a witness, too
to the red-hot kenning
of the Althing.

and when young, we used to turn toward each other,
ink-wet as we were, and ask, 'is this it?'

and I have learned it is, and it was, and it will be.
it is the metronome:

the instantiation
of singular
melody.

and so it is I weep
in the fullness of time
for an epiphany spent too soon.

Don't waste the sun

When it rained, I felt guilty,
Because I remember,
How, when sunlight pierced
The stale brown curtains,
How my father stared
Through me, in a rage,
Until he stopped,
And said:

"Go on then,
Don't waste the sun."

December Rains

dextrous though it is, time fumbles, searching
for silk. Its a woven lattice, can not hold
the white dwarf weight, or the spirit:
a tempestuous broth of crunched leaves,
and, if we lift our eyes: a prelude.

and now my consciousness electric, too,
is a hissing snake in the still brush,
myopia, waist deep in a red lake
of rusted clocks, whose mechanical parts
today count down the stillness they eschew.

and now, lights made of fractal laughter,
in ochre, red, and amber hue, issue sounds
torn from my caterwauling coming into being,
of how i am sundered, and must abjure
as December rain falls.

and here, reddened by rust,
oxygen, and hydrogen combine
to form a ministry of clouds
to remind that time must stop,
and that it already has.

Semantic Hunger

We are one single song in perpetuity,
And death's rigorous palette,
Reformulating ourselves,
Again and again.

We are beautiful crystals until the last,
The connecting,
The concretizing
Form.

But it is only in edifice, and in god
That I might traverse blinding space,
And, as I slip toward erasure
Toward loss,
My meaning is gone in the telling,
And I hunger for what we have left behind.

David Ricchiute

Standing Perfectly Still on the Table

A LIGHTBULB SHINES on bolts of fabric in a kitchen that doubles as a sewing room the boy surveys for a pattern and a ruler. The pattern, somewhere here on the table, is fastened, he thinks, with a safety pin from a basket the last man brought for the mother after she started seeing him. The man before him—the second man?—had a kindly, welcoming way, different from the last man's cynical ways. He took at once to smiling at the mother, smiling at the boy, never once raising his voice to them. That was *nice*, the boy told his mother—the smiling was, the calm voice was—but not till the second man left fed-up and the last man started appearing more, reawakening the sensitive boy to the second man's peaceful ways. The boy knew better than to tell his mother that her smile had faded and her voice seemed tentative, softer, weak.

The first man, a young man—too young, maybe—abandoned the ever-resourceful mother, who long since developed a way with fabric, relying on remnants, instinct, and patterns to fashion for herself, for others, or the boy, clothes she'd assemble at the kitchen table, measured to spec with a yardstick or a ruler, early gifts the first man brought well before his patience gave. Sewing to the boy was an outsized joy, since the mother had begun to rely on him more, particularly on those accumulating days when she seemed to the boy gloomy, low. She had taken to calling him a *trusted apprentice*. "Trusted" the boy had heard before but "apprentice" was a brand new word to him, a word that only a grownup would say, a word that made him feel good.

Tell you what, she says to the boy, who perks up to hear what his mother is saying. *Let's do like they do in a tailor shop.*

Like they do, like what? the young boy says.

This ruler, here, stood on end, makes a hemline guide for a longer dress, like the one we're making now.

The boy wasn't sure what his mother was saying.

I'll stand on the table, the mother says. *You pin the hemline, sitting at the table!*

Why not I kneel on the floor? he asked.

This puts the hem at eye level! The boy's face gleams. *I turn, you pin,* she says to the boy. *I turn, you pin,* she says again. *Place the pins a little bit apart. This much,* she says, holding her thumb and forefinger up. She pulls out a chair from the kitchen table, climbs on the chair to the table top, and motions the boy to sit in the chair. *Gorgeous, the dress you and I will make, like you've heard some of my clients say.*

The boy interrupts to correct his mother: *Our clients!* the young boy says, proud that he got what "client" meant, just like he got what "apprentice" meant—without even having to ask.

Standing perfectly still on the table, bedazzled in a gown of brocade fabric sewn with only a temporary hem from the pattern the young boy found on the table, she shimmies into the top of the dress—the "bodice," she teaches the boy to say—and tells the boy, who's sitting at the table, *Stick on the gown, at the 10s, a pin. Ten inches up, at the 10,* she says. *A pin,* she says. *Straight up, perfectly straight, the ruler,* she says to the timid but helpful boy to whom she's been both mother and father.

The boy hasn't met his biological father and the mother doesn't mention the long-gone man. The boy doesn't mention his father either. The young boy knows, or has come to know, that his father is best unspoken of. Still, he knows, somehow knows, that as time goes by, not just yet, he could ask his mother where his father went and, more to the point, what he doesn't get: A parade of men bound to move in—some nice, most not, like the men with them—why wouldn't a father just live with his kids? Most do, after all.

Turn, the boy says to the mother, both of his hands released from the fabric, and she does—one step—on the kitchen table. Then, *stop!* the boy shouts to the mother, after her two feet come to a rest. She does, she freezes, and he does too, waiting for the sway of the hem to still, waiting to place another of the pins at exactly the height where the last one is.

They were doing well, she told him so, her standing tall, him cautious with the pins. And they will again on another day, if not for hers, then another woman's dress, like the one they're sewing for a mother-of-the-bride, enabling them to afford what they need: sewing supplies, bolts of fabric, rent, utilities, food for the table, and the cell-phone she bought to replace the one the boy heard crash on the bathroom wall but she said merely fell in the floor.

Atop the table at a dizzying height, she scans the kitchen, the walls, the floor, noticing things she'd seen before but now from an angle new to her: a window-valence fraying at the seams, the ceiling stained from cooking oil, the unfinished top of a pantry door. But oddly, given the length of his stay, nothing in the room remains of the first man—by far, the longest to stick around—not even the wall marks she repaired, save for the ruler and the wooden yardstick she struggles at night to uncouple him from. And she struggles, too, independent of him—more now than before, she's come to admit—when the knot in her belly feels heavy, taut, her thin body stiffened from an empty void an article led her to think she's in.

From here on the table, turning her head, she can see in the bedroom to her unmade bed where, huddled in a quilt—groggy, fatigued but short of the restful sleep she needs—she lies awake and succumbs most nights to a dreamful urge: To assume the form of a bird on the wing, taking to flight at the moment of flight, relying on instinct, reflex, whim, to soar at will, to glide unencumbered, to disembody from the weight of herself, an escape from the suffocating tunnel she's in. There's a way, she knows, to disembody but she also knows—the first man taught her—that the trouble with drugs is they work, at first.

I'm glad we'll be alone, he says, returning her to the task at hand and startling her to realize that, without her having said a word, the young boy senses that the last man's going to leave soon, gone with his indifference intact, just like the men before him did. *I'm glad*, he says again to his mother, who reaches into her jeans back-pocket through an unsown seam on the side of the dress.

One more pin, one more, he says, both hands raised from the task at the table.

That's quite enough . . . ., begins the mother, glancing at the hem now circled in pins.

She holds in one hand the brand-new phone and positions with the other the over-head bulb. (*. . . of this*) the mother says to herself, a silent but ever so powerful call to alter the fabric of lives played out at a kitchen table. Phone held high, she aims the camera toward the smiling boy, the first man to seem to understand that this time, again—like every other time—she'll emerge from the tunnel whole again, ushered by the boy who'll become a man.

Both hands holding the hem aloft, she carefully steps from the table to the chair to the kitchen floor, then turns the chair to face the boy. It's cumbersome moving in a pinned-up dress, but she feels the urge to speak to the boy in a way she hopes more tactile than speech. Sitting together, face to face, she leans in slightly, smiles at him, places her hands on the young boy's face, and files his cheeks with her fingertips—a gesture he'll use when the time comes later for another man to raise his kid.

MARVIN COHEN

Loving Candace

LOVING CANDACE

Did I love Candace Watt?
Actually I still do, no matter what.
That was no figment of my imagination.
It was true blue, in the land of sensation.
Is she still available?
Not quite. She can't respond
in the sense that Britain is beyond the pond.
Is she inaccessible?
Maybe, but she's still blessable.
But this sounds too much like a confessable.
To be with Candace, nothing was wrong.
I wish I could set it to musical song.
To be with Candace was positively right.
I wish I could set it in front of my sight
to the full extent of shining light.
Let her be able to confront me
in real life that will shine,
so that she could still be mine,
and I could still be hers
without the defect of blurs
that I get from tears
that cover all those years.

A FREE MAN

I'm a free man now that Candace is dead.
Free to love her more and more
right down to her inner core,
where my love has its great big store.
So many memories are released
in my unwelcome privacy
that her being absent is a piracy.
Why can't she join me at this?
It would contain too much bliss.
My having exclusive exposure
is too secret a disclosure.
She's as free as a bird,

being neither seen nor heard.
We're so unequal,
I'm yearning for a sequel
like a high-gliding mountain eagle
far away from the nest,
and it's not for the best.

WHY BE ASHAMED
TO SUBMIT TO THE DISEASE
YOU'VE NAMED?

Since I'm afflicted with old age,
why should I go into a rage?
It's not my fault that time went by
and disappeared into the sky.
It's neither a sin nor a crime
to be defeated by almighty time.
Don't be ashamed to admit it,
since legal austerity won't forbid it.
Don't be time's self-defeating snob
that you went along with the popular mob
and boasted how long you could hold out
and resist Death's so far undefeated clout.
In the baseball idiom, "three strikes and
    you're out."
If you defy that stern rule,
admit you've been playing dirty pool.

TOO DIVIDED,
OUR GAP WIDENED

Between Candace and me,
I'm the only living one
who's taking advantage,
so I'm the expansive
one, free as a bird
who can be seen and heard,
while she's shut up in death's cage
and can't emerge.
She could be my companion
to roam the wide canyon,
but we're on different levels.
I'm one of the free devils.
She's helplessly out of commission;

and mine is a remembering mission—
for divided couples a tradition.

I GOT A GLIMPSE!
BUT THAT WAS THE WORK
OF IMPS

I dreamed that Candace rose from the dead
to reappear with her old body and head
that were momentarily animated
and virtually uncontaminated.
But it was too good to be true.
So once again she disappeared from view
and frustrated my living self
to rejoin her effigies back on the shelf
as though truly rejected
instead of lovingly expected.
What was real and what was not?
Ruling Death retied the old knot.
Thus my grief reappeared,
and all was left the way I had feared.
Was it a terrible tease?
It certainly wasn't designed to please.

BETWEEN HER DEATH
AND MY LIFE,
I'M IN A KIND
OF MENTAL STRIFE
IN A PUZZLE ABOUT MY WIFE

Candace is dead, and I'm alive,
but our union must survive.
We ended so much together
that the difference between life and death
we managed to weather.
Does that sound mystical?
No. I mean it physical:
I take up her death's slack
by managing to get her back.
She's spiritually mine again,
overcoming difference between now and
    then,
as if her death now regained her life then.

Don't think I'm touched by insanity
to restore her life organically.
Am I taking an unholy liberty?
No, my mind isn't warped. I drink real tea.
Does that somehow reassure me?
No, I'm not going crazy.
It's just that my mind is sort of lazy.

"JOIN ME!" IS
MY HELPLESS PLEA

Being alone while she's dead
brings too many memories to my head,
which we can't share.
It hurts me to be so bare.
I need her to join,
representing the other side of the coin
which has two faces,
so the coin slides.
I need her sharing,
or I can't be bearing
being the sole representative
in our only active world
successfully unfurled.
Oh join me, Candace,
to spread our canvas.
You're the absent one
making me only half done.
We used to have such fun.
It can't be reproduced.
Neither of us can be seduced.
Being halves, we're reduced.
I'm too alone
and bruised to the bone.
I miss you too much,
especially your dear lovely touch.
Let's reminisce
for gossip we miss,
and meanwhile constantly kiss.
You're the part that's missing
for talking and listening
with dashing eyes glistening.

Vincent Czyz

Contrary Star

"I'm a LONG-DISTANCE DRINKER," S. David likes to say. "Just put the bottle down next to me."

When he starts in on claymores and clan rivalries, it's a safe bet he's halfway through it.

He lifts his chin. "Know what a claymore is? It's like a broadsword, only bigger."

We're sitting in a bar in Kearny, a turnpike exit in New Jersey where S. David lives. The floor and the bar, the fancy mirror frame behind it, are nicked-up wood that's bald in ghostly ovals where the finish hasn't held up.

Regular Eddy—tattoos wound around his arm, long hair swaying when he walks—slides off his stool and puts quarters into the '60s-'70s jukebox. Someone else is dinging bells and slapping the sides of a pinball machine, beer mug rocking on top.

S. David is a recurring event in my life without the observable regularity of an eclipse or a comet. Years go by without more than a glancing thought (a sonar ping) then there's a call from a payphone, and he's shouting in my ear to pick him up at the police station or meet him for a drink.

"D'ye hear the pipes, man?" S. David asks. "*Bratach bhan chlann aoidh*. A cry to stir the blood. *White banner of Mckay* is all it means. A proud, belligerent bunch if ever there was."

He pronounces *Mckay* to rhyme with *sky* rather than *way*.

He tells me about a clan known for hundreds of years as a collection of cowards because at the end of a grand battle their last man, thoroughly outnumbered, tossed his sword in a river, jumped in after it, and swam off.

Talking clans, bags, and pipes reminds him of his job.

"The Whirlwind 2," S. David says, "it's not a vacuum, it's a cleaning system. If it wasn't that I inherited my father's Errol Flynn looks, I wouldn't have sold a one."

He's got the pencil-thin mustache and quick eyes (his are blue), the bright smile, and a laugh that makes you think his insides are greased.

Before Whirlwind vacuum cleaners it was a $2,500 water purification system on commission.

"Selling those was like being unemployed only I had to go to work every day." He smiles through cigarette smoke, weather marks trampling the corners of his eyes. "I was a professional visitor."

Generally unwelcome.

Encyclopedias door to door, vacuum cleaners by appointment, magazines over the phone, car phones from an office, Norwegian frying pans guaranteed for life out of the trunk of his rust-and-Bondo Dodge Dart (painted a hideous metallic green), not to mention rubber spiders (a perennial junk prize in boardwalk arcades).

I nod. I know the litany. I'm his oldest friend though it's been mostly radio silence for the last few years. We met in high school, talked wizard spells and *The Earthsea Trilogy* till early morning, idolized a red-eyed albino with wild hair named Elric, who brandished a black sword with a will of its own. We set off after Elric, looking for a Vanishing City somewhere between the Weeping Wastes and the Sighing Desert. Overtired, we half believed we'd made it as dawn seeped into the sky and glazed the lake behind his house pinkish gold.

The sea was S. David's first love. He was out on the lake with a two-man Sunfish, a surfboard with a sail really, before he knew how to swim.

"My great-grandfather, the English one, fell from the mast of a sailing ship off the coast of South America. I come from a long line of drinkers. He was buried near Buenos Aires. We spent years lookin' for the grave."

High school for S. David was four years of cutting classes and collecting detentions, of rolling joints and lighting up behind Krauszer's. A bunch of us hanging out in those sparse woods, passing around the smoldering doobie or quarts of beer.

"What the hell you gonna do with your life, Mckay?" we asked him. "You're smart as the valedictorian, but you're not gonna pass gym class."

"The Navy." He grinned.

Not just a job, an adventure.

"No two days the same. Go to foreign places, meet exotic people, lord it over them, and get paid to do it. Call me McIshmael."

He couldn't wait to get out of Ringwood, the Jersey suburbs, all those porchless single-families lined up along streets without sidewalks.

Years later he's the appliance manager at a K-mart, I'm a copyeditor at a small-time newspaper, and the Navy is a glass-bottomed boat gliding over the past.

"Nine months out of the year, the nearest land was straight down. Four directions all the same. Yeah, I saw the world all right, and two-thirds of it is water." He knocks back a shot of scotch, chases it with a swallow of beer then looks around as if to jump ship.

"Saints preserve us but not ships. Sailors do that, tussling with rust and barnacles, using pneumatic hammers or sanders or just a flat-bar scraper and a square of sandpaper, hands numb from the kind of cold you only find north of the Arctic Circle. The sun sets at 10 pm and comes up at two in the morning.

"Or you'd be in the heat, half blind between the glare off the water and the sweat stinging your eyes, and your shirt can't come off. We used to complain all the time—Hey! Even the Marines get to roll up their sleeves! 'That's the point,' the BM2 Mitchell would say, 'Marines are allowed to. You are not.'

"And then there was sweepers duty, swoosh the standing water off the deck. I was late once, so I had to write over and over again I WILL NOT BE LATE FOR SWEEPERS. A fuckin' grown man, a 2nd class petty officer.

"*A clean ship is a happy ship, I told 'em*, and had a big smiley face for a visual aid.

"After a while, you have to start making things up, the sun scorching your vision and the sound of the ocean *fwoom! fwoom!* against the ship while you sand away forever and a day. I'd wind up taking down an evil sorcerer or two, making the perilous crossing of the Weeping Wastes, somehow or other saving the ship from certain destruction."

He downs another shot. "The Navy's not just a job, it's a cleaning system."

"Huh?" I reached for my mug.

"A machine is what I'm getting at. Steel skin, nuclear heart, sonar ears, radar eyes— whaddid they need me for?"

Boatswain was his position in the log book. *Bozun* is how you say it. Or just *boats*.

"We're what's left from the days of wooden ships and iron men." He winks.

Nights on the weather deck, staring out on moonlit seas with headphones and a microphone. Anything within sight or hearing to be reported. To pass the time, he recited Robbie Burns to the waves.

The fear o' hell's a hangman's whip
To haud the wretch in order
But when you feel your honor grip
Let that aye be your border

"Never saw a giant squid or any a those pop-eyed beasties that're supposed to live below the light, deeper than subs go. I suppose that nuclear-powered mountain a steel I was on would've scare off Moby Dick. Yessir, watch was boring all the way, and I'm only thankful Robbie Burns wrote 12 volumes."

Though he admits an Irish sailor he met in Japan told of a night late as a dishonorable burial when he thought he heard one of those screaming banshees, and he touched the medal of St. Christopher around his neck.

"'It was an eerie sound I doubt any sea thing could make,' said Irish.

"Cheap whiskey'll do it to you every time," I said.

"'Cheap whiskey don't affect me ears, it chews a hole in me gut.'

"I get knots in mine."

S. David's specialty.

"I can make a knot that slides, one that'll never come out, one that's pretty enough to braid a bracelet out of. Got out of the brig once doin' fancywork for an admiral. Two thousand feet of it. I could make about any knot that ever was, but I couldn't take 'em out for shit."

His first love paid for his second: the Navy sent a check home to his 18-year-old wife and unborn daughter. The marriage was a 15-minute ceremony at city hall, six people attending. All the trimmings of a PTA meeting. She'd just graduated high school.

"Lookin' back on it, I think she was rather fond of me spending most of my time at sea and sendin' money.

"In sickness or in health, she said. I don't know which applies, but it's gotta be one of 'em."

One long swallow empties his scotch glass. "You know what she says to me on the way out? I'll always care about you. What does that mean? It means I hope you don't die, but if you're going to live, do it somewhere else."

A woman at the bar is drinking alone. S. David nudges me, tips his head toward her and says, "Nice set, huh?"

"That's what got you in trouble the first time, isn't it?" I ask.

"Caught me young and unawares. An unfair fight from the first."

Never got his high school diploma. Interest wasn't something he could bring to class like pen and notebook.

"Geometry is an odd-sided figure no one uses. History's there for future reference, waiting to be made. English is a figure of speech in a manner of speakin'. Taught me the Greek roots of *disaster—dis* and *aster* . . . *contrary star*. Lot of good it does me when I make a sales pitch."

He puts an arm around my shoulder. "I learned a few things since I saw you a couple years back. For instance . . . marriage, I now know, is a study in knots an' lines. Everything is tied to everything else—you gotta face the Ex if you came to see the kids. All you can do is try to make it come out lookin' nice."

He pulls out a piece of paper, as folded and worn as an old dollar bill. "We been pals since about 1977," he says, "which is forever as far as I can tell. Lemme show you the notes from my AA meeting."

Chemicals used:

Alcohol. Ever since I can remember. Still doing a fifth a day.

Marijuana: Started at 14, last used a week ago. Half ounce a week.

Hash: started at 14, last used about a year ago. Occasional.

LSD: Started at 16; last used 5 years ago. Occasional.

Cocaine: Started at 20, last used last month. Three grams a week.

Crank: Started at 20, last used 2 yrs. ago. Half gram a week.

What happened since high school, I wonder, and summers on the lake dock, where we drank beers Dominick Lasalle bought us. S. David invented the moon dive, baring his ass to the sky as he went under, our clothes littering the planks. The Moon—the real one—was silvery and wavering through five feet of water, through the years that closed overhead. The first wake-up call we got was when S. David went swimming drunk with his clothes on (boots, too) and almost drowned.

The second ding-a-ling, I guess, was the time I found him lying like an empty bottle on the floor of his room, naked, a cigarette burned down to his fingers, his head tilted to the side—still trying to swim with his boots on. His sandy hair longish, his face roughened and darkened by the beginnings of a beard.

I confiscated half a pint of insomnia cure.

Next to his head lay a pen and notebook.

Diary for AA.

10 Mar. I have finally admitted that I am powerless over drugs and alcohol and that my life has become unmanageable and no fun.

11 Mar. I'm not drinking, socializing, or having fun.

12 Mar. I'm reading from the big book AA gave me.

15 Mar. Remembering the past, reading big book, the Bible, and THE SORCERER OF NIKORLANA.

18 Mar. I hate fun.

20 Mar. Everything a man does is for his mouth, it says in Ecclesiastes, but still his soul is not satisfied. Maybe we're spending too much time on the wrong part of the body.

24 Mar. Today I will approach people and talk to them instead of standing there feeling unwelcome.

30 Mar. Unless I fail miserably and repeatedly, I cannot believe that there is something I cannot do.

"Blacking out," S. David explains, "is like losing time. It's there one minute, and the next it's like someone just kept folding it till it's gone. Body's way of outsmarting the mind—it knows you can't sleep an' drink at the same time."

"Nature's crafty like that," I say.

"Ain't it, though? You don't know what you were doing before you blacked out, what you were saying, you just appear again out of nowhere. One day I appeared in a bar saying HEY! WHO STOLE MY UNDERWEAR? I had my dress white pants on inside out. That was Hooker Hill in Seoul, Year of the Turtle. My honor leaked all over me. The cutest call girl in the place—in a dress that didn't miss a curve—sat in my lap and said iloveyoujoenoshit. Then she said she was gonna give me a Korean name. Cheap Charlie because I wouldn't buy her a drink."

"You been outta the Navy for what? Ten years now?" I ask.

"Mmmm," is the best he can manage with his glass in his mouth. "Let me bring you up to date." His glass hits the counter with a *thunk*. "My rent's two months past due, the Ex had me arrested 'cause I ain't been payin' child support, the collection agency is still on my ass for things I can't even remember, and my car refuses to move till its demands for a new alternator are met."

The bartender, a burly biker type with a beard and a mane of black curls, refills his glass.

"On the bright side, Ed McMahon just wrote to tell me I may have already won 10 million dollars."

Somehow he managed to dodge an ulcer, has no heart condition, not even a receding hairline. Always looks the part of imperturbable businessman, his tie in a perfect double Windsor (a simple knot for him). The secret, he says, is to let the reducing valve do its job, don't look ahead more than a day or two.

"Worrying never changed a thing." He empties his glass and motions for more. "Before I let something bother me, I ask myself: Is it really gonna tip the Cosmic Balance? Gravity's still doin' its job, night shows up at the end of the day, and my name's only come up in the obituary column once."

It was a joke his shipmates played on him.

"I don't mind livin' twice, but gettin' married once is more than enough. Nothing worse than calling a place you can't stand home.

"'A wife, a son, a daughter, and what do you do with your pay?' she bitched. 'It goes to the first hooker you see in port, girlfriends in foreign cities you'll never see again.'

"At least I paid for it," I said, "you gave it away.

"'You drank the groceries, damn you. A fence post would've been a better father to our children.'

"I don't doubt it. But you'd look silly with it in your wedding pictures."

He turns to me for absolution. "Nine months at sea, what's a man supposed to do? I never kept a one."

He would tell her he'd certainly look her up first thing back to port in Sterling. First thing in Sterling he took a cab to Perth.

"After a few more of those Unauthorized Drunks, I knew a court martial was comin', so I went UA. Unauthorized Absence, the Navy calls it. FU, I call it. I ain't coming back."

S. David shifts in his seat, adjusting the weight of a leaden past on his back, a certain comfort in the effort of carrying it; he hopes it's making up for something.

"She had a right to blame me, but you know, not once did I hear her say, *It'll be okay, we'll get by*. When I called her from Japan to tell her I'd been kicked out of the Navy, my only dream is sunk, she said, 'What are you going to do now? You got no family to support, you know.'"

S. David sees himself as a man more sinned against than sinning, but I wouldn't want to be the one keeping score.

"I'd already been put down on paper for dishonorable discharge, but the Navy wanted to finish throwing me out, officially, so they tracked me down all the way to Wayne, New Jersey, and took me back to San Diego." He rolls his eyes toward the ceiling in thanks or supplication. "Good thing Dad wasn't around to see it."

He stares straight ahead, not at the bottles stacked against the mirror but at some other reflection. "My grandma turned in her own son, my uncle, for desertin' the army. Honor's redder than blood. Dad used to say *My dignity covers me like a cloak—even if I were naked in the street*. I'd pay $1.50 to see that. He died when I was out to sea. *Och, away with ye lad*, he used to say. That's what I miss most.

"Wasn't till four years after the fact, we four kids and Mom got together to throw his ashes into the Atlantic. He wannad it that way so the part of him that wannad to go back to Scotland would be able to. Left it up to the tides. After the last of him dissolved in the waves, I said, 'Let's throw Mom over and save a trip.'"

Leaning hard on the bar counter, one of his elbows in an old spill, he's maybe remembering standing on the eroding edge of the Australian continent, the universe, his own past.

"Honor's like a vacuum cleaner," S. David says. "Can't force it on people, and nobody particularly seems to wannit. Difference is you can't buy it, can't steal it, can't get it off an assembly line.

"Mac the Moneybag, my grandpa, owned textile mills in India. Depression wiped 'im out. He was forced to lean on a broom t'stay on his feet. Street sweeper in Dundee is what he became. But lemme tell you, when he went t'work, he had on a pressed white shirt, a tie, and pin. He was buried in the same."

S. David shouts, "I WILL NOT BE LATE FOR SWEEPERS!"

Regular Eddy and the woman turn their heads.

"This bottle—" He lifts up his beer. "—always stands by me. Never doubts, never complains, doesn't nag. Makes me forget what's so bad about bein' a failure." He turns to me. "'Course, you can't sincerely ask God for forgiveness for something you're going to do again as soon as you feel better." S. David raises an arm. "Gimme a green flash bartender. A scotch with a twist of sunrise at sea." He winks. "I don't want no rocky road to recovery, give me a nice paved two-laner to hell anytime."

I start to protest, but he cuts me off.

"I know I've got t'quit forever, but yesterday, when I tried, there was half a bottle a vodka in the kitchen. It woulda been a terrible waste a my hard-earned money to let it go down the drain. And the worst of it is liquor stores—those capitalist leeches—take credit cards an' sell to anyone over 21."

"Last call," the bartender says. "Everyone but you, Mckay." He turns to me. "Stick a fork in 'im, he's all done."

S. David tries putting his arms through the sleeves of the jacket hung on the back of his chair, looks like he might fall off trying. "You know what it is? You can be a man of honorable intentions, but there's that contrary star. You steer by it without knowin', you and the Andrea Doria both."

He puts out a hand to give mine a shake. "Havin' gotten used t'the Wife, iss wonderful t'talk to someone who's innerested in what I'm sayin'."

He gets his jacket on without toppling over, slides off his chair, and stands up.

"Much like the waters a Loch Ness, the mind of a Scotsman's so deep'n murky no one's sure what's in it. Works in mysterious ways. If I dredge my mem'ry for a green flash, I can just about see it."

His eyes flicker sapphire.

"You never heard of it? Iss what it sounds like, just before sunrise on an' open sea. A sheet a green light." He spreads his arms slowly, palms down. "Covers sea an' sky but you blink an eye, you missed it. After iss gone, you can't even be sure you seen it. An' what if you haven't? Izzit any different from not knowin' if you never made it to the shore you set out for?"

MIKE SILVERTON

Ten Acuities

THE LEMON WHISTLE

Buy a ticket, sign up, sneak in,
do whatever you have to do,
tell them anything, I don't care,
but don't forget to mention
the lemon whistle.

SAVAGES

Savages tiptoe everywhere
as if transporting lit candelabra.

HIGH WIRE

We salute fine lines delineating nations
in their way like circus high wires.
Were I not an acrophobe, I'd celebrate cartography,
parents shielding their children's eyes.

AUGUST POEM

Gustav Fabergé is lost in thought with a half-dozen eggs,
"Weeping urchins hanging off eaves, smelling like something."

Weeping urchins hanging off eaves, smelling like something

O my swan, how, absent handles, shall we proceed?
(How, too, absent directions?)
The boy stops at the door.
"Gentle door, open, O please do!
No no! I eat so little!"

And the sun, especially yellow that late afternoon,
fulfills a deathbed wish.

Asterisks, fungi, a hint of flailing snails
a voice whisp'ing "Pillage!"

Expressionless mammals standing in snow,
who speaks for them?

That would be me, also recalling unfortunate trysts.
One finds me on tenterhooks,
muttering a leave-taking including bagged edibles.

Creole malaise requires participation.

Sensing no further despondencies, I decommission
and decompose.

Question

The poet imagines nephews colliding with walls.
Do you find this as disturbing as a hangman who says
"Have a nice day" as he pulls the lever?

Zouaves

Take care not to slip on Zouaves rolling around the floor
like small crystal balls.

Sinister Poets

Sinister poets abduct Mrs. Superman. Gadzooks! Banzai!
Sinister poets underscore their demands with the blood of poets they don't like.
Sinister poets whisk Mrs. Superman across state lines.
Explosions follow. "Not our fault!"
Blue skies, blue eyes, Eddie Rickenbacker, immelmanning butterflies.
Mrs. Superman remarks an odor. Nostalgia?
Sinister poets will not hear of it, question her sanity.
"My destiny promises punctures and confectionery slime."
"Nay! Not so!" cry sinister poets. "Let us, rather, nip your mind's skin
with the fleas of our wit. Let us, rather, do the twitchy thing,
which it pleases us to call our facial Monroe Doctrine.
Let us contemplate, rather, a peaceful conclusion in the silence of the page.
We would like to love you."

Boric Acid

An aviator sets out to skywrite BORIC ACID.
Cruise ship passengers observe his plane glinting in the sunlight
as he banks to emit letters of smoke.
Passenger: Is he actually writing BORIC ACID?
Passenger: Maybe. Hard to tell.

A deliveryman who cannot say why
screams "Boric acid!" at a housewife.

A mounted moose head in a modest, dimly lit tavern
bears the legend *Boric Acid* etched on an oval brass plate.

A SWAT team greets liberated hostages with shouts of *Boric acid!*
along with snappy salutes of index fingers to brows.

Daybreak. Borek A-Cid emerges from his yurt.
Moments later he buries his face,
furrowed by anguish, in embroidered throw pillows.

Architectural Feature

An airborne architectural feature lands on one buttress and so remains,
like a lawn jockey. Reverberations throughout the realm,
madmen slamming doors, mermen herding landlocked girls.
As for you, auditing intimacies in your dental fillings,
insanity drowns in conjecture and health in general improves.

Streets under Bridges

Streets under bridges submit to anonymity, in states moreover of liminal anxiety:
the span might collapse, in whole or in part. It happens. No matter.
Tho its street be mysterious, quaint or merely grim,
a bridge's underbelly commands one's gaze. One stands on such a street,
taking no note of condition or direction, imagining jumpers on Christmas Eve.
I have a tooth in the oven.

Language as Form / Language as Music

Lilies on the Deathbed of Étaín and Other Poems
Oisín Breen
Beir Bua Press
Jan 2023

When I went to the crematorium, I saw him,
    Godstruck
And his was the face of God,
And that lamenting voice, his too
That song of skin sung to the pilgrim's heady
melody.

Oisín Breen is not a poet shy of recapitulating his national poetic and literary tradition—he imbues this collection with a uniquely Irish melodious cadence and draws heavily upon the riches of Irish mythology, which he sprinkles into almost every stanza. In a way, these poems become ballads, a story set to a music that seems to have been passed down through generations but is made anew every time a new voice joins in. Though Breen's words are written, the balladic nature of this work makes it seem to exist outside of codification, in a place where new meanings can still seep in.

In the introduction, Breen emphasizes the theoretical underpinnings of his work, commenting on how he studies "the relationship between the complexity paradigm and narratology" at the University of Edinburgh as a PhD candidate. If, in reading that statement, you asked, *what the hell does that mean*, I want you to know that I asked myself the same question. As far as I can tell, it means he's trying to find where the idea of "even in chaos, there is order" intersects with how we frame narratives and use narrative language to express internal thought processes. In other words, how do we capture our thoughts, which can be sporadic and temperamental and jumbled to the point of confusion, in a way that reveals a shared meaning.

I think.

And if that was the author's intention, *I think* he's captured it in an interesting way. There is a lot of stream-of-consciousness poetry out there and this isn't that. There is an explicit story or scene. But there isn't a straightforward arc. Rather, this writing mirrors another famous Irishman, James Joyce, and fluctuates between the narrative voice(s) and time. These techniques can be jarring in less skilled hands but Breen manages to pose these moments in opposition to each other so that when we read:

He fell.
Motherless.
Motherless.

He fell.
And I have never seen anything so beautiful.

we are unsure if the 'he' and the 'I' are distinct personalities, or in fact that same person.

In work that is so heavily imbued with references that are probably not too well-known outside of Ireland (Who is Étaín? Answer without Googling), the reader will enjoy its sonic quality, how it complicates identity, and the inherently symbolic nature of each piece. Lilies, for example, placed on a deathbed are a really interesting choice, given their role in Easter and the idea of rebirth. The apostrophe in the central poem is made to a preternatural holy woman, a creator, who is surrounded by "bright red fruit", from whom Christ is "cleaved", "a forest flush with birth". Her absence is counterbalanced by the vivid and original descriptions that make her omnipresent in the speaker's, and thus the reader's, mind. So do not let unfamiliarity with Irish folklore deter you—the highlights here crown a beautiful collection whose magic lies within its language, its feeling, and its song.

> This wet soil, from which I fashioned you a
> sleeping coat,
> It is heavy with meal-worms.

> This heat of yours, it will fire my body,
> This instrument of lilies.

Writing as Living Document / Writing as Memorial

Survivor's Notebook
Dan O'Brien
Acre Books
Sept, 2023

Dan O'Brien's *Survivor's Notebook* is a beautiful little hybrid book that calls itself poetry, though the paragraph-length entries inside are more memoir or, at the very least, are reminiscent of confessional poets like Robert Lowell or Russell Edson. The collection spans all four seasons and ends by circling back to Spring, which, for a book about cancer, seems very meaningful. Perhaps it's not fair to call this a 'book about cancer', though there certainly is a lot of it in these pages. It's probably more accurate to say this collection is about the aftermath of survival, its memories and lingering questions.

The book open on Good Friday and the image of Christ follows O'Brien silently through his documented year. In the background, the reader sees a discarded hospital gown like the shroud of Turin, there's a terra cotta bust of Madonna, and, by the end of Fall, he's in Jerusalem. O'Brien isn't a Christ-figure though; instead, these Christian elements act as counterparts to the lengthy existential questions he asks himself and to his pervasive doubt. For many who undergo trauma, G-d feels far away. As O'Brien reminisces about a time where a play of his received no reviews and he thinks "maybe it's true that nobody is really watching but you." At another point, he says "I prefer NED (medical speak for "No Evidence of Disease) because remission reminds me of sin." Though he distances himself from faith, it is always there, following along. The reader sees its influence, silent but steady throughout this work.

And if G-d is always there, lurking just out of reach, so is health (or its absence). In the passage "Now", O'Brien states definitively:

> Everybody has cancer, everybody has had cancer, everybody will survive. Everybody will die of it; or something . . . Must I get a real job now? Must I become bored again? Meanwhile the forever war drags on.

Indeed, this seems true as he catalogues all of the people that he's encountered throughout his life, loved ones to strangers, who are eventually diagnosed with various types of the disease. The amazing rates do make it feel like an inevitability. To make matters worse, "[w]orry, my mother said, caused it . . . The more you worry about it the more you make it occur." Loudly, cancer menaces the reader and their narrator throughout these pages, with harrowing images of "doom-dim afternoons of the languishing months in the bardo of chemotherapy [, t]he static nebulas vibrating in the cobwebbed corner of my sickbed."

This is a very honest work. There are personal phobias and fears, secrets and longings exposed. Memoirists—how do they do it? Expose themselves to strangers? O'Brien seems to answer this question by saying that his "mother seemed to imply as she handed me a pen: *You cannot cry to me so cry to them.*" He reflects on his "unspeakable almost cellular sense of humiliation" but is still able to examine painful memories, outside of his mortality, things that live on, like his family's issues.

In as many ways as writing is a living document as long as it's observed, it is also memorial. O'Brien says that wanting to write it all down can be an excuse, a reason for living. So can reading. Particular gems in this collection include: "Motherless 1 &2", "The Cup", "Sunday", and "Kite". Part celebration, part extrication, fans of personal stories about imperfect lives will enjoy this brave and bittersweet book.

> O may it be Sunday always and everywhere in
> California . . .
> The enlarging bright aperture of sand . . .
> The mountain snows dribble from a drainage
> pipe like the seminal Jordan. Seagulls alight as
> if to say, *Look where you are standing. For this you
> have survived.* Our daughter laughs as she pummels us both. O may it be always and everywhere now.

A COVID Collaboration

There is Only One Ghost in the World
Sophie Klahr and Corey Zeller
Fiction Collective 2, Oct. 2023

> You have our unmailed letters. You have your
> addresses of the dead.
> You have a view, a contagion. You imagine a
> body bare and undazed,
> look at your empty hands. The days peel out like
> copies.
> *Copies of copies.*

As someone who runs a small press, I have encountered quite a few manuscripts with the same conceit as *There is Only One Ghost in the World*, wherein two author collaborate on the same piece to stave off COVID ennui. Something inside me is hesitant to invest in these works because it feels like more time is needed to really understand what happened (is happening?). Like the dearth of books about Sept. 11 in its immediate aftermath, it feels like we need some time to properly evaluate the past few years. However, this work isn't a contemplation on COVID itself. Rather, *There is Only One Ghost in the World* uses COVID as an impetus to explore existential questions. Sophie Klahr and Corey Zeller's book reads like a hand-off of notes between two friends, sharing memories and sad stories from their lives as they contemplate existence and our fragile mortality.

There is no traditional narrative arc here; instead, it is a patchwork of impressions. A half-sister kills her donkey; a lover tries to explain constellations; wandering thoughts about pangolins, post-it notes, and porn stars. What separates this from other works that seem like a series of non sequiturs is the authors' use of language. These pages are littered with beautiful moments. In a story about finding baby mice that had fallen from the rafters, one of the authors imagines the mother mouse "sleeping in her somewhere, holding at least one of the lives she made." Another particular favorite:

> Someone tells you that Brian Wilson wrote "God Only Knows What I'd Be Without You" to impress his father. His father wasn't impressed. Years later, he went to see his childhood home and there was only an overpass, and the shambled dirt all overpasses hold beneath them. The arc of eulogy. You want to put a heron in the eulogy, an egret. A living shape that stills the sky.

And another:

> The kid with leukemia who sat in front of you would pass you the pictures they drew. Stick figure drawing a stick figure. Stick figure drawing a house. You drew your own body and passed it back. One day the kid was a solid. Later a gas. Then he evaporated. *This*, the teacher said, *is how you make a cloud.*

We look for meaning in randomness and I found moments of serendipity in these pages.

The vignettes start with first person or third person perspectives but shift somewhere until almost every passage becomes second person. I was taught that second person perspective creates a sense of intimacy between the reader and the speaker(s) but, to me, it seemed to do that opposite here—*you* seems distant, *you* is not me. *You* operate in ways imagined but always unknown to the speaker. *You* and I are apart, in distance, in COVID isolation, in ultimate understanding. There were also repeated subjects in this book, most notably in the form of a donkey. Towards the beginning of this collection, a woman kills her donkey in a story that questions mercy and at the very end, there is a story about a blind donkey named Stella. Stella struggles to survive but ultimately her carers realize that she appreciates music, 'dances' to it. These animals suffer but they both experience beauty, the first through its friendship with a sheep and Stella through her remaining senses. These donkeys represent all living things, whose life is struggle punctuated by moments of joy. *There is Only One Ghost in the World* feels very much like two people living through something, and it's convinced me that analysis can be fruitful at all points in a crisis, even in the thick of it.

REVIEW | M.J. NICHOLLS

Later Stories
Alexander Theroux
Tough Poets Press, Nov 2022

THE latest in Tough Poets Press's heroic unleashing of a lifetime's worth of unpublished manuscripts finds Cape Cod's premier sesquipedalian in typically uncompromising form with a new collection that encapsulates the least appealing elements of his maximalist style.

Opening story 'Rolf Vowels' presents an uproarious caricature of a Cockernee villain—a racist, homophobic thug with an encyclopaedic command of street slang and a voice that is wildly inconsistent—one moment he's using American terms ("freak crazy"), the next he's using obscure words for cunnilingus ("gamahuching"), the next he's coining portmanteau insults ("lunchbuckets", "fudgemonkey"). In far-right Britain, where racist rhetoric is spewed frequently from politicians' mouths, the onslaught of hate speech from this little shit sticks awkwardly in one's craw, likewise the excruciating path to redemption via Jesus that concludes the tale.

'The Ratmansky Diamonds' is flat-out antisemitic and at no risk of being misunderstood as satire, un-PC comedy, or anything approximating humorous. The story concerns a wealthy Jewish couple named Ratmansky (rat man—tee-hee!) besotted with precious diamonds, who secrete their spoils on a farm in bottles of garlic paste before fleeing to America at the start of the Second World War. While in America, they become incredibly fat, feeding their rapacious Jewish appetites with tucker and moolah (of course), all the while stressing over the safety of their prized minerals in war-torn France. An acrobatically kind reader of this abomination might argue Theroux is intentionally mining antisemitic stereotypes to create a wildly off-colour lark that wields the most outrageous and offensive tropes for the shock LOLs. Either Theroux is tone-deaf to the cultural sensitivity of a Christian man revelling in antisemitic tropes, or he's merely interested in tickling his own funny bone—and there's no denying a wild time was had writing these absurd caricatures and making them the fools of the piece—with no subtlety or knowing winks to hidden intentions behind the story. This is a catastrophically tin-eared misfire that honks of the writer's weird unchecked bigotry and lack of any editor politely beseeching him to reconsidering letting this carbuncle ever leave the bottom drawer. (Later in the collection, Theroux address and discusses anti-semitism, making the purpose behind this oddity more baffling.)

Although accusations of misogyny are routinely lobbed at Theroux, the female character skewered in 'An Interview with the Poet Cora Wheatears' is a worthy hate-sponge—an arch, absurdly condescending lady poet who patronises and corrects everyone with whom she comes into contact, a vintage Dickensian grotesque who dismisses Marianne Moore as "cuckoo", Ezra Pound as "twaddle", and categorises John Ashbery, Stanley Kunitz and Jorie Graham as "comb jellies—lower than ctenophores." Successfully managing to plant trivia on poets such as Wallace Stevens into the story in a way that is unbothersome and woven into the comedic tapestry of the tale, this is a classic character portrait-cum-assassination in the manner of 'A Wordstress in Williamsburg' from *Early Stories*, where Theroux perfected this form.

As the collection continues, Theroux struggles to suppress the part of him that is perpetually perched over an encyclopaedia, beaverishly hunting for novel factoids and even more beaverishly eager to share those factoids to anyone who will listen. 'The Corot Lecture' is a lecture on French landscape painter Jean-Baptiste-Camile Corot with fictional baubles included where the lecturer admonishes his students and alludes to his divorce—flimsy contrivances to pass this lecture off as a legit story. (The lecture itself is typically erudite and interesting—should have been plopped in a trivia volume, though). Similarly, 'Revelation Hall' features a young girl oppressed by her religious tyrant of a father who retreats into a private realm of reading and factoid-hunting, allowing Theroux to blitz the pages with random trivia, slowing down and strangling the momentum of the fairly bleak and unremitting story which comes to an abrupt end when he runs out of ways to crowbar in the nous. As one of the few admirers of his trivia volumes (even superfan Steven Moore who wrote *A Fan's Notes* has little patience for those) *Einstein's Beets* or *The Grammar of Rock* et al, keeping the two forms separate would make for a less irritating reading experience, especially when the stories in this monstrous volume average over sixty to seventy pages each.

'The Brawn of Diggory Priest' retells the early days of the Mayflower settlers—a more narratively appealing way in which Theroux imparts learning into the fabric of a historical yarn. 'Envenoming Junior' is the collection's stand-alone WTAF moment, an acerbic rant in which thinly veiled versions of his long-loathed brother Paul Theroux and nephew Marcel Theroux are savaged in an epic litany of beef and qualm, an exhausting roster of everything that has upset Theroux about the other Theroux over the years, leaving him the most isolated of the Theroux dynasty. As a sustained piece of fictional familial evisceration, the story is pretty impressive in its unburdening of grievance, and deserves some kudos for the audacity of its assault, but the tone of the tale is much too bitter and arrogant to scale any artistic heights, and represents the worst of this tendency toward unfiltered spleen-venting that is funnier in other works.

Limping onward through the volume, this reader eventually fled in sheer exasperation. 'Madonna Pica', a story about teens pranking in a seminary has some of the most subpar prose on a sentence level in the collection, forcing me to bail early and skip 'The Missing Angel' and 'The Nemesis of Jawdat Dub', stories that at a glance repeat this tired formula of outlining a character solely for the purposes of flaunting erudition. The final two shorter stories 'Acknowledgments' and 'A Note on the Type' are whimsical canapés lighter in tone, where Theroux flexes his lexical bicep in brief. While this collection is disappointing and the poorest of the three short fiction reissues from Tough Poets Press, it's worth reiterating the breadth of Theroux's knowledge, and the power of his prose style where the possibilities of language are boldly exploited as by no other writer out there today. As a prose artist, Theroux crafts stories that are passionately in love with words and their potential to thrill and excite the reader. Alas, his previous peaks of prose mastery mean these lesser forays stick out in a canon of uniformly astonishing work, and so are deserving of the serial whipping that this reviewer has performed—entirely out of love and admiration.

For those eager to explore Theroux's fictive world beyond the novels, I'd recommend *Early Stories* as the most essential of his story collections.

REVIEW | David Kuhnlein

F20 Grail 12
CJ Christine
Expat Press, 2022

F20 GRAIL 12 resurrects a dead zeitgeist to butter up our own, a kind of controlled choke outside time. Christine's book combines ASCII art with minimalistic free verse, a neon-printed nineteen-nineties sky pressed in cake. Silent dialectics manifest, be-costumed nylons a-swish, toward a biology cut from nature with a dull blade. Embossed participants seem to reach through the cover.

Christine dedicates the book to "Victory. Each necrosis of a poem sparkles in her enemies' wounds. Candy karat limos, prayed on posers, coffins full of candlelight—it is a Marilyn Minterian femininity decorated with codeine. This is the end of art for art's take. The author's sins will be rewarded again.

Modified ideal in miniature, the root of disease can work as a non-sequitur. Excerpted below, prepositions compete: "round" slaps its surplus on "over." Both come ungoverned and over-governed within a sonnet that shot every couplet. "My tractor old timey little thing / little peasant bus, that's my diamond ring"—smoldering friction.

As soon as the sun sets
and the dust settles on the road
soon as the crows stop buzzing over round my
    villa
soon as Morgellons symptoms
stop strangling my mother

In his essay "On Contradiction" Mao Ze Dong writes, "Without contradiction nothing would exist." He refers to social classes, but this theory is also adapting ancient Chinese philosophy: a fusion of polarities, yin and yang, dark and light, male and female. "If there were a God, I'd pray that he hear me and I pray he be a man," Christine opines, not without irony. Opposite facets of a single thing must exist simultaneously for growth to occur. Mao refuses to believe in an art spat from the void, bearing, at least, results crafted from tradition, even if we'll abuse him here to communicate with angels. The opposing worldview, Mao also notes, a timeless, metaphysical outlook, "regards all things in the universe . . . as eternally isolated from one another and immutable." The speaker in Christine's poem "pebble coffin" might agree:

> On the internet
> with roses and velvet
> I'll lay there
>   open casket
> ....
>   forever and ever

Christine understands decadence, degradation, and crime as occasions for glory. "I'd sip espresso / with an AK47 in my lap . . . Christian Violence, I'll accept it." And Christine is involved in a self-transfiguration, a self-realization. "What about me? Well, I had a perm in 1984." Through non metered lines, Christine frees herself from self-deception, and is engaged in a dialectic of freedom. Immersing oneself in a book of poems, then, could be thought of as purposely drowning in the author's ocean of their perfect subject. "Help me drown, drown my entire account," she writes in one poem. In another: "Stay right here and watch my tractor / I'm gonna tie you up right after."

With contemporary technique—poem as joke, poem as internet cheat code—Christine teases familiar pleasures. Nothing didactic, more a roving admonition. Her poem titled, "If I had a gun" is a follow-through jest: "You'd all be dead." Aesthetic dimensions giggle freely. Another fun one-liner is "Parakeets": "I'd buy 20 and shoot 19 just to test their loyalty." Later: "Have you even learned to mewl yet . . . Does the road ever end when you're the only one you know?"

AI might meme us back to life. Remember *Big* with Tom Hanks opening on a kid glued to his computer, standing in the evil witch's cavern, surrounded by the carcasses of slain ice dwarfs? The cursor blinks green. Our hesitancy will cost us dearly.

The Lost and the Blind
Curtis Smith
Running Wild Press, 2023

When living on the edge isn't a choice, it isn't really an edge—rather, it's a state of dispossession. Such is the situation of Mark Hayes, the central character of Curtis Smith's sixth novel, *The Lost and the Blind*. He's a high school senior and caretaker to his junkie mother and her likewise addicted friend, whose infant child also requires Mark's attentions. Mark is the sort of kid who "wasn't destined for the world of little league practices and doctors' appointments and getting to school on time." His father is in prison, and Mark fits the profile of a likely candidate to follow in his footsteps.

But he is self-aware and chafes at the routine disrespect and indignities that his mother experiences, the profiling that exacerbates her woes. He wants nothing of it, or of The Patch, the drug-ridden neighborhood where he grew up, and where the rest of his community appears all too ready to consign him, to keep him "out of sight, out of mind." Torn between loyalty to his mother and to self-preservation, Mark walks a fine line.

Smith's earlier novel, *Lovepain* (2018), was narrated from the point-of-view of a husband dealing with his wife's addictions. In *The Lost and the Blind*, Mark tells his own story, with the relative powerlessness and vulnerability of a teenager. Here, for instance, he considers his mother's pain, and the price of her chosen remedy:

> Only the needle lifts her from the tide. Each dose a rapture and rescue. Her first waking and last drifting thoughts a calculation of when she'll fix again. Her greatest desire to

shut out the voices of the present and past and have a final say-so in a life where she's had none. But this erasing of the world is a sloppy affair, and in the process, she's erased jobs and bank accounts and a man or two who could have been good to us. And when her eyes roll back and the needle slips from her fingers, I understand she's erasing me too.

This passage is fairly representative. Stylistically, Smith favors short chapters and punchy sentences; he often elides verbs. Events move along briskly. At the same time, he allows space for introspection, for Mark's awareness of the gravity of events.

And, for all the darkness, there are also moments of tenderness, of solidarity, as well as glimpses of a wider world of hope. Mark befriends a blind neighbor who awakens in him a deeper interiority; he does contract labor for Chief, who serves both as a father figure and as a source of cash, which, in light of the material realities of Mark's world, where the refrigerator is often empty and meals get missed, is no small affair. He slowly develops a relationship with Kate, a girl in his class, despite the distractions of home that preclude any clichés of teen romance.

A particularly memorable section of *The Lost and the Blind* recounts Mark's improvised Christmas and its harrowing aftermath, which includes a raid by ICE authorities, a snowstorm, and a visit to his father in prison. Mark's choices, good and bad ("reason is a luxury"), are circumscribed by his hometown but they are also placed against a larger backdrop of an America at war abroad, with its news cycle of bombing missions and hostages. Military recruiters roam the hallways at Mark's high school. Joining the army might be his only escape, even if it could thrust him into situations more violent than what goes down at The Patch.

Curtis Smith has created a poignant and complicated protagonist, whose plight goes far beyond a sentimental plea, like a 21st century Oliver Twist, for more soup. (Though there are occasions when he could certainly do with more soup.) In addition to the problems of material injustice, *The Lost and the Blind* also evinces a strong spiritual longing. Throughout the story, well-intentioned people (and some not so well-intentioned) try to appeal to Mark with formulas of piety or scripture, and, although these efforts don't convince him, because they don't jibe with his experience of the world, he appreciates their attraction, to those lucky enough to have known otherwise. His soul hungers.

I'm reminded of a pivotal scene in W. Somerset Maugham's *Of Human Bondage*, where a stingy vicar, who is the uncle of the young protagonist Philip Carey, makes a magnanimous show of offering him the top of a boiled egg. The boy would gladly eat the entire egg, but even in his stomach-growling disappointment, he wonders about his uncle, too, about what is the matter with the man, what makes him behave this way, what must ail his soul.

Smith conjures up an similarly powerful moment when Mark collects money for a contracting job at a doctor's house. Serious personal problems over the holidays resulted in the job getting finished one day late.

> He opens the envelope, and inside, a fanning of green, but before he hands it over, he removes two fifty-dollar bills.
>
> "The work was promised to be done by the 30th. That was our agreement." He pockets the bills and hands me the envelope.
>
> I hold the envelope. I think about the bills inside—and the ones he made a show of removing.

It's not only about the money, though the money is very important to someone like Mark, who doesn't have enough of it. The doctor has performed a territorial act, drawing a line, keeping people like him in his place. Later in the story, when Mark puts himself in risky circumstances, the action haunts him.

I can't shake the image of the doctor pinching those bills. Because he made a show of the subtraction, wanting me to see who had the power.

Fast-paced, psychologically subtle and sometimes disturbing, *The Lost and the Blind* is a gripping novel. It is both empathetic and unsentimental: generous in its conception, and potent in its art.

Debra Di Blasi

Epistles of the Unsaintly

(an ekphrasis, after Pieter Bruegel's *In the Land of Cockaigne*)

0:1*

"Dark matter has consequences. If it wasn't there, we wouldn't be here."
—Peter Higgs, particle physicist

What in heaven

were you doing, expelling us from paradise?

We were all photons and light waves. Safe in a state of perpetual becoming. Swimming fecund on the nib of your pen in the tangible moment a drop of ink gathers, swells, and then—

ah, such blessed *nothing*: a stasis extravagant as an oily rainbow bent round creosote. No hunger or thirst, no needless need for the golden bidet or fob, nor the bloated blowfish of a man's ego—cock equally engorged while a greased palm strokes it.

The cock crows.

Sun's mounting white temples.

No sleep for the wicked!

Good god, we were dreams not dreamers! Particles colliding in copulation, conceiving bosons. Yes, yes! Giving birth to god-particles—aphid honeydew on your eyelashes. And when you blinked, when the quasars throbbed . . . Ecstasy!

1:2*

"They are going to kill everything. Everything is dying. We are all going to go hungry, the children will be hungry, my daughter will be hungry, and I'll be hungry too."
—Pire'i Ma'a of the Awá-Guajá Tribe, Amazon Rainforest

What on earth

were you thinking, handing paradise back?

Cakes and ale, bacon pie, pangolin stew, broomsticks on the backs of orphans. We're addicts slumped in soporific stupor; we belch and snore. Our blood's saltier than tears, than oceans rising, than crust on a dead seahorse crushed under heel. We shit ground beef patties and fries. Fart hotly. Love the smell of grease in our pimples, wax in our ears, cock juice in juicy cunts. *Finger lickin' sniffin' good.*

Oh, stop complaining! We're your epithets. We fashioned language from the shit you made of us, forged between snout and anus, teeth and balls. Every tongue's a cancer. Every windpipe's a storm.

Ink drops. Felled rainforests burn and become *caatinga*—white weald—and peccaries flee. *There's* your crown of thorns, you fascist. *There's* your golden calf worth its weight in golden tribes going extinct: 300 leftover Awá move deeper into the Amazon and drop like meat tossed to pariahs, like flies on rotting meat, like sated maggots swarming ochre corpses. Tomorrow there are no Awá, no jungles, just a wide river of white mud and no regrets.

> *O Fortuna!*
> *Monstrous and empty, you spinning wheel.*
> Tamarins convulse; the peccaries will not be back.

3:5*

"My perspective is the Earth will be here. It just may not be habitable to our life form.
We get confused. We think we're the center of everything."
—Mae Jemison, NASA astronaut, engineer, and physician

What in hell
did you hope would happen, except hell on earth?

> You and your cocky wagers. Your lazy gaze. Wasn't it our *right* to be untethered, blinded by our resplendent grotesque, to slog through desert sands until our kidneys ached and our piss ran red? Wasn't it our *privilege* to die, for chrissake, under the Eternal Banyan Tree. Bellies so bloated our skin ripped wide open. Viscera spilled. Hearts exploded like red poppies blooming on the Fields of Flanders.

> Goddamn it, you ceded! Surrendered your power and punishment. And now *you-know-who's* squatting up in the treehouse, out of reach, while we shudder in shadows, fat asses on plumped pillows of worms. We're revolting.

>> Does it matter, our remorse?
>> If we string him up—the one who's kept us down—
>> will the sins of our fathers then make breaking news?

No, no, no. It's *his* bloody knife, *his* plastic platter o' plenty, *his* sinking boat steered by slippery fish waiting for fins to become limbs so they can walk on water and out of it, straight into the hairy present, onto lands they'll ravage until—

Jesus Christ, those dying oceans! Those fast-fading peoples and myriad carbon organisms stuck in the muck of our glut. Can't you hear The Adversary laughing his wild peccary snort—slurping suet, sucking marrow, masticating torn gristle.

We'll eat each other, finally. Gnaw bloody hangnails down to bone. We'll roast umber babies on a spit over hellfire and brimstone and none's the wiser. None's the crueler.

8:13*

"In this inferno of intense heat, the Earth's atmosphere would vanish in minutes,
its oceans boil away in hours, and the Earth itself evaporate in a few years.
And yet, when we survey the heavens, we find the universe plunged in darkness."
—Edward Harrison, *Darkness at Night: Riddle of the Universe*

What in God's name,
hidden behind bruised palms, do you want from us, anyway?

What was the point, after all? The universe expands. Stars go nova and comets burn in blue ellipses. Spiral nebulae collide and coalesce. Those of us who love beauty are governed by those who loathe it, who swing their cudgels till our eyes pop out of our charred skulls. Led blind by the seers of darkness, we've nowhere to go but back to the beginning, before *in the beginning was the word,* when you took up your pen and sucked on it an infinite while, brooding, until a flood of ink turned your tongue indigo and you drowned.

Ashes. Eggshells. Gallnuts. Schoolhouse glue boiled from hooves. Once we prayed in rhymes. Once we believed we could reach you just beyond the fractal hemline where you sat humming some *Swing Lo'* hymn that would bring us all home.

Once, we believed.

> The Adversary's squatting in your luxury condo.
> He put his name in gold on your golden gates.
> Says he owns you and cannot be evicted.

21:34 . . . *

"The infant universe was a creature of heat and light, but the cosmos
of the ancient future will be a dim, cold animal."
—Paul Sutter, astrophysicist, "The Universe is Dying. Now What?"

Where, oh *what* in the world
is *You* but dormant in background haze?

Varnish dims and darkens. Narratives change: Some dumb art restorer wiped out the passenger pigeon. And you! You're long gone in the vanishing point of our one-point perspective. Symmetry's nothing but the repudiation of life, the cancelling out of old debts and dreams. At the end of a Hadron collider is another collider. Another god nodding off in blissful sfumato, bleeding needle dangling red from the crook of an arm.

> Tangled in a *Fibonacci sequence* is a *thinglessness*
> dazzling as a Roman coin in muck, hoary as anthrax in blood agar.
> *Nothing* hums like a pledge of wasps louder than you.

Our time's coming—don't wait for us—it's going, surely as we'll become godforsaken photons pummeling transcendent retinas, no more than electrical impulses in the chiaroscuro of pen on paper. Blink once and we're gone.

JOYREADERS

That SPRING, the essay "Ah, Did You Once See Borges Plain?" was found missing from the pages of *Exacting Clam 11* while the issue was being proofed. Editor Sigh Becker called the police, and they assigned the case to a literary detective—a magnifying glass in a leather jacket—who studied the scene and declared the essay stolen. "Look," said the detective, studying the new space between pages 19 and 23. "See these frayed edges? These pages were torn fast." The magnifying glass put his hands on his hips. "Probably joyreaders."

"Joy-*readers*?" Sigh said.

"They read for fun, skimming mostly, then ditch the essay somewhere and move on to another." The magnifying glass squinted. "Let's *hope* that's the case, at least—and that it's not the alternative."

"What's the alternative?" said Sigh.

"Just hope it's joyreaders," the detective said.

The police didn't have any luck tracking down "Borges," though, and a week later another selection was stolen from Issue 11: the poem "n00b b00n." The same magnifying glass arrived to survey the scene, but this time they brought along a colleague—a second magnifying glass, this one bearded and smelling of cigars. "I know this is frustrating," said the first glass, "but the work may still turn up."

"How's your security?" said the second magnifying glass.

"Security?" said Sigh.

The second glass looked to the first, and then back at Sigh. "I'd beef up my security if I were you."

Two days later, happily, "n00b b00n" was found ditched in a nearby lake. The poem was waterlogged, though, and one of the phrases therein—"common safari habits"—was bent and dented and needed to be replaced.

The police had less success finding "Ah, Did You Once See Borges Plain?". The editors checked with the magnifying glasses weekly, but they rarely had any new leads. The essay wasn't found until a month later, when it was recovered—along with about twenty additional missing poems, stories and essays stolen from other books and journals—in a raid on a literary chop shop. The essay had clearly already been parted out, though; some sentences had been reduced to single words, while other paragraphs had been reconstituted into new, senseless sentences: "Borges . . . perhaps was born . . . and died," for example, or "My question was . . . another . . . Rainbow" and "The goal is . . . wondering." The essay's author, Kurt Luchs, was beside himself, but he and the editors immediately set to work rebuilding the essay—a painstaking process that took weeks.

In the meantime, Sigh had taken the glasses' advice and posted a help wanted ad for a security booth. He received several applications, and the booth he hired was energetic and eager. While Sigh'd asked him to simply stand fast at the copyright, the booth insisted on patrolling the issue in full. He'd shine his flashlight on any corner of the page that seemed suspicious, and interview every reader he encountered to make sure they were reading slowly and responsibly. Never again, the security booth promised Sigh, would Issue 11 have to worry about joyreaders.

Contributors

si Bender is an artist from Upstate New York. She elms KERNPUNKT Press, a home for experimental riting. She is the author of *KINDERKRANKENHAUS* M, 2021) and *The Book of the Last Word* (Whiskey Tit 19). Her shorter writing has appeared in *The Rumpus*, lit Lip, *Adroit Journal*, and others.

J. Blumenthal, an American writer in Munich, Ger-any, writes in both German and English. He is the uthor of a non-fiction book on feral man, *Kaspar ausers Geschwister* (Kaspar Hauser's Siblings), and a erman-language blog, "Der Sprachbloggeur."

evin Boniface, an artist, writer and postman in Hud-ersfield, West Yorkshire, UK, is the author of *Sports and cial* (Bluemoose Books, 2023), *Round About Town* (Uni-rmbooks, 2018) and *Lost in the Post* (Old Street Pub-hing, 2008).

hristopher Boucher is the author of the novels *How Keep Your Volkswagen Alive* (Melville House, 2011), olden Delicious (MH, 2016), and *Big Giant Floating Head* MH, 2019). He teaches writing and literature at Boston ollege and is Managing Editor of *Post Road Magazine*.

ish poet Oisín Breen's work is published in 89 jour-als in 19 countries, including in *About Place, Door is a Jar, orth Dakota Quarterly, The Tahoma Literary Review*, and ew Critique. He is the author of the collections *Lilies on e Deathbed of Étaín* (Beir Bua, 2023). *4² by 5* (Dreich, 22), and '*Flowers, all sorts in blossom . . .*' (Dreich, 2020).

egan Catana (formerly Schikora) is a Michigan na-ve with work forthcoming in *Midway Journal* and *F(r)ic-on*. Her short fiction and creative nonfiction can also e found in *Fictive Dream, New South, Flash Fiction Maga-ne, The Rumpus, The Literary Review, Foliate Oak Literary agazine, Flyway, BlazeVOX*, and *The Crooked Steeple*.

nn Cefola's Sanguinetti translations include *The Hero hax Press, 2018) and *Hence, this cradle* (Seismicity Edi-ons, 2007). Ann is also author of *When the Pilotless Plane rrives* (Trainwreck Press, 2021), *Free Ferry* (Upper Hand ress, 2017), and *Face Painting in the Dark* (Dos Madres ress, 2014); and recipient of a Witter-Bynner Transla-on Residency, and Robert Penn Warren Award se-cted by John Ashbery.

arvin Cohen is the author of many novels, plays, and ollections. His latest book is *How, Upon Reflection, To Be morous* (Sagging Meniscus, 2023).

incent Czyz is the author of collections of short fic-on and essays, two novels, and a novella. His work has ppeared in *Shenandoah, AGNI, The Massachusetts Review, outhern Indiana Review, Tampa Review, Georgetown Review, n House*, and *Copper Nickel*, among other publications.

ebra Di Blasi is an artist and award-winning author f 13 books, most recently *Birth of Eros*, a novel. Her rose, poetry and hybrids appear in anthologies and urnals of innovative literature. She is a former pub-

lisher, educator and art critic now dividing her time between the US and Portugal.

Dave Drayton was an amateur banjo player, founding member of the Atterton Academy, and the author of *British P(oe)Ms* (Beir Bua), *E, UIO, A: a feghoot* (Container), *A pet per ably-faced kid* (SOd Press), *P(oe)Ms* (Rabbit), *Haiturograms* (SOd Press) and *Poetic Pentagons* (Space-craft Press).

Daniel Felsenthal is a poet, fiction writer, critic and essayist whose work has appeared in *Pitchfork, the Village Voice, Artforum, Los Angeles Review of Books, The Baffler, Kenyon Review, Frieze, The Believer, BOMB* and elsewhere. He is also Assistant Editor at the literary annual *NOON*.

Jack Foley's numerous books of poetry, fiction and crit-icism include *Visions and Affiliations*, a "chronoencyclo-pedia" of California poetry from 1940 to 2005, *Grief Songs* (SM, 2017) and *When Sleep Comes* (SM, 2020). He lives in Oakland and hosts a weekly radio show, *Cover to Cover*, on Berkeley's Pacifica station, KPFA.

Jake Goldsmith is a writer with cystic fibrosis and the founder of The Barbellion Prize, a book prize for ill and disabled authors. He is the author of a memoir, *Neither Weak Nor Obtuse* (SM, 2022).

Tyler C. Gore's essays, stories, and reviews have ap-peared in many of the fine, high-quality journals pre-ferred by discerning readers like you. He is the author of *My Life of Crime: Essays and Other Entertainments* (SM, 2022), a delightful book that you should definitely buy. He lives, as he dreams—in Brooklyn.

Henrietta Goodman's fourth collection of poetry, *Antil-lia*, is forthcoming from University of Nebraska Press in spring of 2024. Her poems and essays have been pub-lished in *Poetry Northwest, Bennington Review, River Teeth, New Ohio Review, Gulf Coast*, and other journals. She teaches at Rocky Mountain College in Billings, Montana.

Tomoé Hill is the author of *Songs for Olympia* (SM, 2023). Her work has appeared in such publications as *Socrates on the Beach, The London Magazine, Vol. 1 Brooklyn, 3:AM Magazine, Music & Literature, Numéro Cinq*, and *Lapsus Lima*, as well as the anthologies *We'll Never Have Paris* (Re-peater Books), *Azimuth* (Sonic Art Research Unit at Ox-ford Brookes University), and *Trauma: Essays on Art and Mental Health* (Dodo Ink).

Jesse Hilson is a freelance reporter living in the Catskills in New York State. He has written two crime novels and a book of poetry.

Charles Holdefer lives in Brussels. His latest novel is *Don't Look at Me* (SM, 2022).

Nick Holdstock is the author of two novels, *The Casual-ties* (St Martins, 2015) and *Quarantine* (Swift, 2022), and a short story collection, *The False River* (Unthank, 2019). He has written three non-fiction books about China: *The Tree That Bleeds* (Luath, 2012), *Chasing the Chinese*

Dream (IB Tauris, 2017) and *China's Forgotten People* (Bloomsbury, 2019).

Glenn Ingersoll works for the public library in Berkeley, California. Videos of his poetry reading & interview series *Clearly Meant* can be found on the Berkeley Public Library YouTube channel. His prose poem epic, *Thousand*, is available from bookshop.org and as an ebook from Smashwords. His poem "Personal Testimony" was given a Special Mention in the 2022 Pushcart Prize anthology. Poems have recently appeared in *Crowstep Journal*, *Thieving Magpie*, and *The Sparrow's Trombone*.

Akshat Khare is an Indian novelist and poet. He is the author of *Delhi Blues and Other Poems* (2020), *The Book of Saudade* (2023), *Truth Be Told: A Tragedy in the Making* (2023), and *Signifying Nothing*.

Kent Kosack is a writer, editor, and educator based in Pittsburgh, PA. His work has been published in *Tin House (Flash Fidelity)*, the *Cincinnati Review*, the *Normal School*, *3:AM Magazine*, and elsewhere.

Richard Kostelanetz is an American writer, artist, critic, and editor of the avant-garde. He survives in New York, where he was born, unemployed and thus overworked.

Alvin Krinst, legendary *Urdichter* of the American literary underground, is the author of *The Yalta Stunts* (SM, 2016), a translation of Dante's *Inferno* (into limericks), the novel *No Smoking*, the poetry collection *GIGFY*, the ballet *The Jazz Age of Haroun Al-Rashid*, and many other works. He divides his time between Quito, Ecuador and Reykjavik, Iceland.

David Kuhnlein is the author of *Die Closer to Me* (Merigold Independent), *Decay Never Came* (Maximus Books), and his horror film reviews are collected in the zine *Six Six Six*. He edits the book review column *Torment*, *venerating pain and illness* at *The Quarterless Review*. He lives in Michigan.

Ben Libman is the author of *The Third Solitude* (Dundurn Press, 2025). He lives in Paris.

Kurt Luchs is the author of *Falling in the Direction of Up* (SM, 2020), *One of These Things Is Not Like the Other* (Finishing Line Press, 2019), and the humor collection *It's Funny Until Someone Loses an Eye (Then It's Really Funny)* (SM, 2017). He lives in Michigan.

Niamh Mac Cabe is an Irish visual artist and writer of fiction, nonfiction, poetry, and hybrid prose. She's published in many journals and anthologies including *Narrative Magazine*, *The Stinging Fly*, *Mslexia*, *The Offing*, *Southword*, *No Alibis Press*, *The Irish Independent*, *The London Magazine*, *Aesthetica*, *Lighthouse*, and *Structo*. She's won many awards, including the Wasafiri Prize, John McGahern Award, and Molly Keane Award. She lives in Leitrim, Ireland.

DS Maolalai has been nominated eleven times for Best of the Net, eight for the Pushcart Prize and once for the Forward Prize. His poetry has been released in three collections, most recently *Sad Havoc Among the Bir* (Turas Press, 2019) and *Noble Rot* (Turas Press, 2022)

Melissa McCarthy's *Photo, Phyto, Proto, Nitro* is pul lished by SM in Nov 2023, following 2019's *Sharks, Deatl Surfers: An Illustrated Companion*. She has been here in Ed inburgh, playing right wing-back. More at sharksillus trated.org.

Jim Meirose's work has appeared in numerou venues. His novels include *Sunday Dinner with Fathe Dwyer* (Optional Books), *Understanding Franklin Thompso* (JEF), *Le Overgivers au Club de la Résurrection* (Mannequi Haus), and *No and Maybe—Maybe and No* (Pski's Porch).

Róisín Ní Neachtain is a writer and artist living in Ki dare, Ireland. Her work has been exhibited in grou and solo exhibitions most notably in Riverbank an Cultúrlann in Belfast. Róisín recently finished a men torship with Brian Maguire.

M.J. Nicholls' most recent book is *Violent Solutions to Pot ular Problems*. He lives in Glasgow.

Paolo Pergola is the author of *Passaggi—avventure di u autostoppista* (Rides: The Adventures of a Hitchhike (Exorma, 2013), *Attraverso la finestra di Snell* (Throug Snell's Window) (Italo Svevo Edizione, 2019), and *Res* (SM, 2021). His work has appeared in several Italian li erary magazines. He is a member of OPLEPO/Opifici di Letteratura Potenziale (Workshop of Potential Litera ture), Italy's equivalent of France's OULIPO. He lives i Tuscany and works as a zoologist.

REYoung is the author of *Unbabbling* (1997), *Margarii and the Snowman* (2016), *Inflation* (2019), *The Ironsmith: Tale of Obsession, Compulsion and Delusion* (2020) and *Zi* (2020). He continues to reside in a limestone cave dee below the city of Austin, Texas.

David Ricchiute is the author of a story collectior *Keeping What's Best Left Kept Secret* (Cornerstone Pres 2024) and two poetry collections, most recently *Uncer tain in the Worst Way* (Main Street Rag Press, 2020).

Hélène Sanguinetti is the author of *Domaine des englue* (La Lettre Volée, 2017); *Et voici la chanson* (Lurlure, 2021 reprinted from L'Amandier, 2012; *Le Héros* (Flammar ion, 2008), *Alparegho, Pareil-à-rien* (Comp'Act, 2005 ; sec ond edition L'Amandier, 2015), *D'ici, de ce berceau* (Flam marion, 2003), and *De la main gauche, exploratrice* (Flam marion, 1999).

Mike Silverton is the author of *Anvil on a Shoestring* (SM 2022), *Trios* (SM, 2023) and the forthcoming *Geront Abecedary*.

Guillermo Stitch is the author of the novella *Litera ture™* (2018) and the novel *Lake of Urine* (SM, 2020). H lives in Spain.

Thomas Walton is the author of *Good Mornir Bonecrusher!* (Spuyten Duyvil, 2021), *All the Useless Thing Are Mine* (SM, 2020), *The World Is All That Does Befall U* (Ravenna Press, 2019), and, with Elizabeth Cooper man, *The Last Mosaic* (SM, 2018). He lives in Seattle.

Printed in Great Britain
by Amazon

33415417R00067